Hereford

History and Guide

Hereford as it was in the early
seventeenth century, before the
Civil War. A model in the Old
House Museum

Hereford

History and Guide

Ron Shoesmith

ALAN SUTTON

First published in the United Kingdom in 1992 by
Alan Sutton Publishing Ltd · Phoenix Mill · Far Thrupp · Stroud
Gloucestershire

First published in the United States of America in 1992 by
Alan Sutton Publishing Inc. · Wolfeboro Falls · NH 03896-0848

British Library Cataloguing in Publication Data

Shoesmith, R.
  Hereford: History and Guide
  I. Title
  942.466

  ISBN 0-7509-0191-8

Library of Congress Cataloging in Publication Data applied for

Cover illustration: Cathedral and Old Bridge, Hereford (Viewfinder
Colour Photo Library)

Typeset in 10/13 Times.
Typesetting and origination by
Alan Sutton Publishing Limited.
Printed in Great Britain by
The Bath Press, Bath, Avon.

Contents

Acknowledgements

I would like to record my most grateful thanks to the following people and organizations without whose help this book would never have been written. To the Hereford Branch of the County Library, and especially Robin Hill, for access to and permission to use their large collection of prints and photographs; to the Hereford City Museums, and especially the curator, Anne Sandford, for permission to copy and use both prints and paintings of the city; to the Hereford Branch of the County Record Office, and especially Sue Hubbard, for permission to copy and use documents and paintings in their collection; to my employers, the City of Hereford Archaeology Committee, for permission to use material from their records; to the many authors of the various articles on Hereford in the Transactions of the Woolhope Naturalists' Field Club who have provided much essential information; to Ken Hoverd, who produced the excellent photographs used in this book, often from old prints and glass-plate negatives in poor condition; to Dick Vowles, Martin Knight and Ken Hoverd, who all read early drafts of this book and provided many useful comments; to my publishers, for their understanding and good nature; and to my wife and two children who had to tolerate me throughout the production of this book.

ILLUSTRATIONS

The sources of the various illustrations used in this book are as follows:

Hereford City Museums: pp. 14, 15, 30, 37, 56, 68, 70, 80, 82, 88, 91; **Hereford County Library:** pp. 4, 5, 12, 21, 31, 33, 38 (upper), 39, 49 (lower), 50, 52, 65, 66, 89, 90, 95, 96, 99, 102, 110, 111, 112; **Hereford County Record Office:** pp. 28, 57, 94; **Hereford Archaeology Committee:** frontispiece, pp. 10, 11, 13, 32, 38 (lower), 47, 48, 49 (upper), 53, 69, 74, 76, 105, 109.

Introduction

I n 1989, Hereford celebrated the 800th anniversary of the granting of the first Charter to the city by King Richard I in 1189. A few years earlier, in 1976, the cathedral had a similar celebration – in this case the 1,300th anniversary of the founding of the diocese in 676.

The history of urban settlement in the area goes back to a much earlier date, and the predecessors of Hereford can be found in the Roman town at Kenchester and the Iron Age hill fort at Credenhill, both some 8 km west of the present city.

No single book could ever do justice to the 2,000 years or more of history and change that has made Hereford what it is today. In this work I have tended to concentrate on the development of the city, events which have caused changes to the basic plan, and the design and variety of its buildings.

For many years Hereford was a frontier town on the border of Wales. As such it had a significance to the defence of the country which far outstripped its modest size. Most early kings were regular visitors and its castle was one of the strongest and most impressive in the realm.

After the conquest of Wales, Hereford became a quiet market town, remote from the rest of the country. The lack of any good means of communication was to affect the growth of the city for many years, and the many and varied methods of resolving this problem are integral to a proper understanding of the city as it is today.

A city is created as much by the people who have lived and worked in it as it is by its position and external events. I doubt I have given them the prominence they deserve. The past inhabitants of Hereford have made decisions, rightly or wrongly, which have made the city what it is today. Their contribution should not be forgotten.

To Ben & Katy
who have asked many of the questions –
I hope this book provides some of the answers

CHAPTER ONE

Hereford's Predecessors

Thereere is little trace of any permanent occupation in the Hereford area before the Iron Age. This is probably because most of the Herefordshire plain, which is associated with the rivers Wye and Lugg and their tributaries, was heavily wooded. Most of the evidence for early man during the Neolithic and Bronze ages comes from the higher ground in the south-west of the county. Surface finds, such as polished axes and flint arrowheads, which have been found occasionally in the Hereford area, are more likely to have come from hunting expeditions rather than being evidence for any permanent settlements.

There was a radical change at the beginning of the Iron Age, which in Herefordshire can be dated to the sixth century BC. This was the age of the hill-forts – large camps with massive ramparts, which are a feature of many of the hill tops throughout Herefordshire and the Welsh borders. At least half of the camps in Herefordshire are over 6 hectares (10 acres), the largest being at Credenhill, some 7 km (4^1/$_2$ miles) north-west of Hereford. This is roughly central to the Herefordshire plain and it has been argued that it was the hill-fort capital of a geographical region similar to the old county of Herefordshire. If this is correct, it is within the ramparts of this Iron Age hill-fort that we must look for the origins of urban settlement in the Hereford area.

Credenhill was probably constructed about 390 BC. This was a time when there was much reorganization of the local hill-forts into larger units with new defences in the form of inturned entrances with timber guard-rooms. At its peak, the population of Credenhill could have been as much as 4,000 – a sizable proportion of the 25,000 estimated population of Herefordshire at that time.

The hill-forts are easy to recognize because of their massive defences, but the extent of tree clearance for grazing and cultivation in the surrounding areas is much more difficult to assess. Trees would have been cut down for building purposes and for fuel, and grazing would have helped to prevent regeneration. During peaceful periods farms would have been built outside the defences and one such was

1

recently excavated on the lower ground to the south of Credenhill. It was eventually replaced with a Roman villa-farm complex although there was no evidence for continuity of occupation.

The limited archaeological excavations at Credenhill in 1963 give a tantalizing glimpse of the potential importance of this massive hill-fort. The 20 hectares of gently sloping ground enclosed by the defences is slightly larger than the well-known hill-fort at Maiden Castle in Dorset. The massive rampart was derived from an external defensive ditch and from an internal quarry ditch. The external slopes vary from 1 in 5 to 1 in 3, producing an excellent natural defence against attack. There were at least two gateways, to the east and south-east, and there could have been others. At these gates the ramparts turn inwards to create a narrow defensive passage. The excavations were mainly within the quarry ditch area, just to the south of the east gate. The remains of several oblong buildings, each about 3.5 by 2.4 m (12 by 8 ft) and considered to be dwellings, were found. The buildings were probably single-storeyed, with raised timber floors and a ridge roof which could have been thatched. They were arranged in rows about 4.5 m (15 ft) apart.

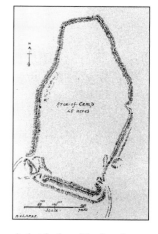

A sketch plan of the Iron Age hill-fort at Credenhill, drawn in 1882

The Iron Age inhabitants of Herefordshire, with their capital at Credenhill, may have been a sub-tribe of the Dobunni but could possibly have been the Decangi, mentioned by Tacitus and conquered by Ostorius Scapula in AD 48. If this identification is correct (and the evidence is very tenuous), the Scapulan invasion of Herefordshire would have been a punitive expedition for it was partly a consequence of invasions by the native tribes into the then Roman province. The archaeological evidence tends to support an invasion of this nature in Herefordshire – the rectangular huts at Credenhill were apparently dismantled; at Croft Ambrey in the north of the county and Midsummer Hill in the east the huts were burnt; and at Sutton Walls, only a short distance north of Hereford, the many skeletons found buried in the western entrance may be evidence for a massacre. The few Roman pottery sherds found on Credenhill need not be later than AD 70 and may represent little more than scavenging within the deserted settlement.

Apart from one quern stone, there are no finds from the area of Hereford city which can be attributed to the Iron Age. In 1931, Alfred Watkins suggested that slight earthworks which can be seen on Aylestone Hill could be the remains of a hill-fort, but nothing has been found to confirm this theory.

The Romans would doubtless have dealt with this unruly area in the same way that they did in other parts of the Empire – with a massive military presence involving the construction of strategic forts and a permanent road system. By AD 80 there were legionary forts at Caerleon and Chester and intermediate forts adjoining the main road which linked them, as far northwards as the River Severn. It would not have been long before the border area was made secure and the civilian powers could then start to take over from the military rule.

By this time the hill-forts would have been abandoned and their inhabitants dispersed. Many would have been taken as slaves – the more fortunate ones would have settled on lowland farmsteads, agreeing to provide the tribute necessary to keep Roman rule flourishing. The scene was set for the foundation of towns, villas and the full panoply of civilized Roman life. Imperial policy would have dictated a centre for tax-gathering and government in each of the old tribal areas, a centre which would also help to assimilate the tribal hierarchy.

The postulated hill-fort capital of the Decangi at Credenhill may well have been replaced by a Roman fort, built on the plain between the hill-fort and the river Wye although evidence is lacking. Such a fort would only have had a short life and would have been replaced in turn by a civilian settlement. This was the walled Roman town at Kenchester, the second predecessor of Hereford. It is the *Magnis* of the Antonine Itinerary and, despite its name, was small by Roman town standards. The defended area of nine hectares consisted of an irregular hexagon with a long axis running west–east. Oddly, the main crossroads was to the east of the town, a little way outside the position of the east gate.

Magnis is now a grassy field but early visitors saw much which is now buried or lost. Leland in the early sixteenth century noted that 'The place wher the town was ys al over growen with brambles, hasylles, and lyke shrubbes. Neverthelesse here and there yet appere ruines of buyldinges, of the which the folisch people cawlle on the King of Feyres Chayre. Peaces of the walles and turrets yet appere . . . and more should have appered if the people of Herford town and other therabowt had not yn tymes paste pulled down muche and pyked owt of the best for there buildinges.'

Other seventeenth-century antiquaries recorded that 'A vault was opened with a tessellated pavement and . . . a hypocaust about seven feet square with leaden pipes entire and some pipes of brick, a foot long and three inches square, let artificially into each other.' 'A vault from which urns were taken with bones and tesserae.' 'A piece of what was probably a temple, with a niche which was five feet high and three broad within.' Stukeley, writing in 1722, mentions 'A very fine

The site of *Magnis* from the air looking west. The line of the main road which ran through the town can be seen

mosaic floor a few years ago was found intire, soon torn to pieces by the ignorant vulgar.'

Excavations in 1913 and 1925 exposed a long section of the main road through the town and the foundations of several buildings. The road was well laid with stone drains on each side some 9 m apart. Buildings fronting the road had wooden or stone porticos or verandahs, and one may have been a temple or public building. Set back from the main west–east road were several large buildings with elaborate mosaic pavements, while the 'King of Fairies Chair' and associated hypocaust and drains probably belonged to a public bath house.

Further excavations on the defences in 1956 and 1963 provided more information about this provincial Roman town. *Magnis* probably started as a roadside settlement laid out along the west–east road. About AD 150 the town was remodelled and earthwork defences and timber gateways were built. The more important buildings discovered during the early excavations probably date to this period. Late in the fourth century the defences were rebuilt in stone with large double gateways and bastion towers. By then the town had all the appearance of a small administrative centre and the remains of several villas and farmhouses which have been found in the neighbourhood indicate the settled nature of the whole area.

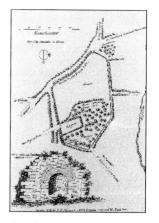

Stukeley's 1772 plan of *Magnis*, the Roman town at Kenchester. Inset is a drawing of the niche called the 'King of Fairies Chair'

The pillar bases of a verandah or portico fronting the main street at *Magnis* which were excavated in 1924 (Watkins)

Part of a mosaic pavement
found at *Magnis* in 1912

Magnis was still functioning close to the beginning of the fifth century when one arch of the eastern gateway was deliberately blocked. The final occupation, as with many Roman towns, is difficult to date. It will need much more detailed archaeological work before it is possible to confirm Leland's hypothesis that 'of the decaye of Kenchestre Herford rose and florishyd'.

There is no evidence to indicate that there was a Roman settlement of any kind close to the ford across the River Wye at Hereford. Although there are good reasons to suppose that the Romans made use of this ford, there are very few finds of the Roman period from some twenty-five years of major archaeological excavations in the city. The few coins found were all in later levels and need not relate to Hereford at all. Two Roman altars were reused in the construction of two seventh- or eighth-century grain-drying ovens, found close to Victoria Street when the ring-road was being built in 1968. A larger altar was found near St John Street in 1821, and a small bronze figurine of Hermes was found many years ago behind the Eignbrook Congregational church in Eign Street but has since been lost.

Such finds do not necessarily provide evidence for Roman occupation in the area. However, the altars are reasonably large and heavy and it would be rather surprising had they been brought all the way from Kenchester in preference to smaller, more easily transportable stones. These altars and the statuette could indicate the presence of a temple or roadside shrine in the Hereford area. Such buildings were often associated with road junctions or natural springs. There was at least one Roman road junction in the immediate Hereford area, and the gravel terrace close to the Wye contained several springs including the Pipewell, close to Gwynne Street, and St Ethelbert's, close to the castle. Alternatively, the altars could have come from a roadside cemetery – a not uncommon Roman feature.

One possible reason for the lack of any major Roman finds in Hereford may be because archaeological work has been very limited in the central part of the city – the areas adjoining the main streets and the ford – and it may be that a shrine, temple, or series of buildings associated with the river crossing remain to be discovered. Even so, it is very unlikely that such buildings would have had any effect whatsoever on the eventual siting of Hereford. It is far more likely that the eventual choice of the site was due to the presence of the ford, a well-drained gravel terrace, and the continuing use of the old Roman road network well after the end of Roman rule.

During the early Roman period the main north–south road, which joined the important legionary fortresses at Chester and Caerleon, probably crossed the Wye by one of the Hereford fords. It would not have been long before a bridge was built south of Kenchester, some 8 km upstream of Hereford. The bridge was probably built of wood and, after the collapse of the Roman Empire, it would gradually have fallen into decay and eventually collapsed or been destroyed by one of the floods for which the Wye is notorious. Without the necessary techniques to rebuild the bridge, the only alternative would have been to divert the road back to the nearest convenient ford crossing – that at Hereford. Thus, possibly during the fifth or sixth century the site of Hereford would have taken up a degree of importance as the recognized crossing of the Wye for people travelling up and down the Welsh border.

CHAPTER TWO

The Early City

I t is very unlikely that we shall ever know precisely why and when a permanent settlement was first built on the gravel terrace adjoining the Wye ford at Hereford. The problems are twofold – there is very little documentary evidence, and what there is tends to be rather obscure, and the archaeological remains are inevitably slight and often difficult to interpret and date with any degree of reliability due to later disturbances.

Attempts have been made to establish that a battle fought in AD 548 at a place called *Fernlega* was actually at Hereford but there is insufficient evidence. There is also a tradition that Hereford was an early centre of British religious activity and that it may have been the seat of a bishopric of the kingdom of the Magonsaete. This is based on the list of seven bishops who, according to Bede, disputed with St Augustine in AD 601. It includes the bishop of Caerfawydd which, it is suggested, could be Hereford.

One other possibility is that the origins of Hereford as a religious centre should be sought on Castle Green, downstream of the cathedral, where there was a pre-Conquest collegiate establishment, eventually dedicated to St Guthlac. It is possible that this was the site of one of the ancient Welsh 'clas' churches, and as such could have pre-dated the formation of the Hereford diocese.

The foundation of the Hereford diocese, although not necessarily the cathedral or the city, is usually considered to date from AD 676 when Sexwulf, the Mercian bishop at Lichfield, granted a church and land to Putta. Putta, who had previously been bishop of Rochester, heads the list of bishops of the western Hecani in early manuscripts. However, there is no independent confirmation that Putta's seat was at Hereford. The area occupied by the western Hecani is rather uncertain but probably equates broadly with the Hereford diocese.

William of Malmesbury described a fine stone cross which he saw in Hereford around 1125. It had apparently been completed by Cuthbert, who was bishop of Hereford from AD 736 to 740 before being elevated to Canterbury. The cross commemorated the construction of a new burial place for the three prelates who had gone before him, together with Milfrith, a prince of the western Hecani, his wife,

Cyneburgh, and 'Oshelm, son of Osfrith' who is otherwise unknown. Significantly, there is no mention of the body of Putta. One possibility is that the early bishops' seat could have been at Leominster, which was founded in *c.* AD 660 by Merewalh, the father of Milfrith. Was it during the lifetime of Walhstod, Cuthbert's predecessor and the originator of the cross, that the bodies of the rulers and bishops of the western Hecani were transferred from Leominster to the new cathedral at Hereford, or was the removal much more local – from the religious foundation on Castle Green to a new church near the present cathedral?

The earliest documentary evidence for a cathedral at Hereford is in AD 803 when Wulfheard describes himself as *Herefordensis Ecclesiae Episcopus.* The monastic establishment of St Guthlac's is not mentioned until *c.* AD 975 but the evidence obtained from archaeological investigations on Castle Green has shown that this is a much more ancient site than the documentary records would suggest.

Castle Green, the site of Hereford castle, is now a pleasantly landscaped area laid out with public walks which were once described as being 'esteemed superior to any other walk of the kind in the Kingdom'. However, beneath the well-mown turf lies buried some 1,300 years of fascinating history.

When the Nelson memorial was built on the Green in 1809 human remains and military weapons were found. In 1886, when a main sewer was laid through the Green, 'the excavators had scarcely gone a couple of feet before they came across human remains. Then, going a little deeper, a whole skeleton was found, and, at a depth of 2 ft 6 in from the surface, three skeletons were found, laid within rude stone slabs, formed into three coffins, each 7 ft 6 in long. Each skeleton measured over 6 ft.' Further observations in the 1920s and '30s were sufficient to suggest that the whole of the southern part of the Green had been used as a cemetery at some time in the past.

Archaeological excavations in 1960 and 1973 confirmed this hypothesis when some eighty-five burials were exposed and examined. Radio-carbon dating has established that the cemetery was in use from about AD 700 until the early twelfth century. Calculations based on the density of the burials and the known area of the cemetery indicate that between 7,000 and 15,000 individuals were buried in this area in the period before the castle was even built.

The excavations also exposed the stone foundations of two buildings. The earlier one was apparently a mortuary chapel which could have been built as early as the seventh century and was probably demolished before AD 1100. It is likely that this building was part of the early ecclesiastical settlement which was later dedicated to St Guthlac.

St Guthlac died in AD 714 and was buried at Crowland in Lincolnshire. His tomb was enriched by King Aethelbald but, when Crowland was destroyed in AD 870, the relics of the saint were apparently dispersed. Perhaps it was at that time that the monastery on Castle Green received a substantial part of the saint's body and as a result took on a new dedication.

The evidence from the archaeological investigations is sufficient to indicate, with a reasonable degree of probability, that the religious settlement on Castle Green was established either earlier than the accepted date of the foundation of the diocese in AD 676 or within the half century after this date. It is possible that the site was chosen because of the proximity of the nearby spring which, at a later date, was said to possess miraculous powers as St Ethelbert's Well.

It is reasonable to suppose that by the middle of the eighth century at the latest, Hereford contained two religious settlements on the gravel terrace overlooking the Wye. Apart from these establishments, there

Archaeological excavations on Castle Green in 1973 exposed remains of St Guthlac's monastery and an extensive collection of burials from the Saxon cemetery

St Ethelbert's Well in the mid-seventeenth century. The masonry probably dates from the fourteenth century

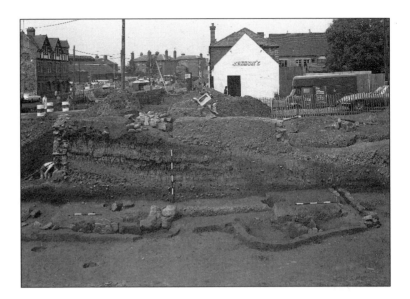

Eighth-century grain drying ovens in front of a section cut through the Saxon defences of Hereford during excavations in 1968

may have been a few houses close to the central crossroads, but the embryo town did not stretch as far west as the present line of Victoria Street. The remains of the grain drying ovens, which were found here in 1968, were dated to this period. They were apparently isolated features in an otherwise agricultural area where oats, wheat and barley were grown.

It was either Offa, during his long reign as King of Mercia (AD 757–96), or one of the minor kings who followed him, who was responsible for Hereford's growth to become a planned royal town. In AD 760 the Welsh were defeated at the battle of Hereford and before the beginning of the ninth century the line of the Welsh border had been stabilized by the construction of the great dyke which bears Offa's name. The dyke is absent from Bridge Sollars, 10 km west of Hereford, as far as Monmouth. Here was the friendly, although autonomous state of Ergyng or Archenfield which stretched from the Wye up into the Black Mountains.

Offa is said to have had a palace at Sutton, 6 km north of Hereford, where, in AD 794, he apparently murdered Ethelbert, king of the East Angles. After miracles were performed at Ethelbert's grave at Marden, his remains were moved to Hereford and he became the patron saint of the cathedral. Because of the murder, tradition has Offa as a lavish benefactor of both cathedral and city.

Archaeological excavations have indicated that streets and houses, planned and laid out on a grid system, were built in the western part of the city at some time between the mid-eighth and mid-ninth centuries.

The single-storey buildings were constructed on earth-fast posts and averaged 6 m wide and perhaps 12 m long with a central cross-passage. They had simple earth floors and central hearths and faced onto a street parallel and west of the present Berrington Street. Each building was in a square plot of ground with sides averaging 18 m long, corresponding to a possible density of fifty properties to the hectare (twenty to the acre) – reasonably generous in today's urban terms. This lost street, together with Berrington Street, Aubrey Street, Broad Street, Church Street and St John Street, forms the visible grid pattern of the Saxon town. They are all bounded on the south by the main west–east road and the cathedral precinct but their northern limits are as yet uncertain. Modern Broad Street, the major north–south road, almost certainly led down to the ford across the river. There is no evidence for any defensive works associated with this early planned town which seems to anticipate the planning of the Wessex *burhs* by at least half a century.

At some time about the middle of the ninth century the main part of the city was enclosed with a gravel bank and ditch. This defence, which enclosed some thirteen hectares, did not include the St Guthlac's monastic site, and was apparently associated with a reduction of the previously occupied area.

The close of the ninth century was marked by a renewal of Danish raids, particularly on the Welsh kingdoms. It was about this time that Hereford's defences were completely rebuilt and extended to enclose

The shallows in this 1898 photograph mark the position of the Saxon ford across the River Wye. The warehouses in the foreground were built for goods awaiting transport by boat down the river (Watkins)

St Guthlac's. The new work, which was well built and designed to appear impressive, probably took place during the reign of King Alfred (871–901). A line of vertical posts, 1 m apart, was set in post-holes a short distance back from a deep ditch. Behind them layers of turves were laid to form an embankment. As this rampart grew in height, split logs were laid one on top of another between the posts and the turf pile. When completed the face would have been about 4 m high including a breastwork. A reconstructed section on the eastern side of the city, behind St Owen's Court, shows how impregnable this would have been.

A few years later the timber works were replaced in stone, probably during the reign of Edward the Elder (901–25) or Athelstan (925–40). This stone wall was probably about 2.5 m high and 2 m wide and was built of uncoursed rubble in front of the existing timber face. The timber breastwork doubtless continued above the top of the wall. The rampart would have been used as a fighting platform and, for ease of access, a 2 m wide roadway was built to the rear of the embankment. It is apparent that, with these defences, the foundation of the Hereford

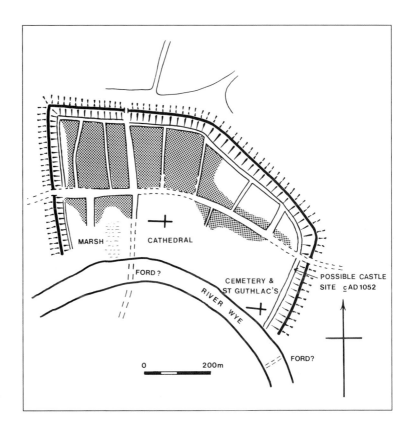

The defended area of Hereford in the early tenth century. Much of the early street pattern shown on this plan still exists

mint, and the rebuilding of the cathedral, the city had become an administrative, commercial, and ecclesiastical centre and was quite capable of hosting a meeting of the king with the Welsh princes in AD 930. The assertion that Hereford 'sprang to glory during the reign of Edward the Elder' would appear to be well justified. Even the design of houses had improved – the new buildings being of timber-frame construction on sleeper-beams, a system which, with minor modifications such as the use of stone footings and fireplaces, was to continue in Hereford until the seventeenth century.

At least a hundred years of relative peace followed and the defences were allowed to fall into disrepair. However, the city must have been relatively prosperous for the built-up area began to expand outside the defences and the cathedral was rebuilt between AD 1030 and 1040 by Bishop Athelstan.

The peace was not to last and in AD 1055 the city was attacked by Gruffydd ap Llewelyn who, according to the Welsh Chronicles, 'returned home with manie worthie prisoners, great triumph, and rich spoils, leaving nothing in the town but blood and ashes, and the walls rased to the ground'. The new cathedral was apparently stripped of its valuables and may have been damaged but not totally destroyed, for a year later when Bishop Athelstan died his body was brought to Hereford and buried 'in the church which he had built from the foundation'.

After the sack by the Welsh it is recorded that Earl Harold returned to Hereford 'which he forthwith fortified with gates and bars and with a broad deep ditch'. The Anglo-Saxon Chronicle is somewhat less specific – 'Earl Harold had a ditch (earthwork) made about the town during that time'. The actual extent of the work is debatable; it was certainly not a time for expansion, so he probably strengthened the by then decayed Saxon defences, clearing out the ditches and reconstructing the gates. It was not until well after the Norman Conquest that Hereford fully recovered from this attack.

Coins of Edward the Confessor (1042–66) from the Hereford mint

CHAPTER THREE

Norman Expansion

T he purpose of the Domesday survey, which was carried out during 1086, was to establish 'what or how much each land-holder held . . . in land and livestock, and what it was worth'. The Commissioners had also to establish the changes which had occurred since 1066 – it was meant as an authoritative record of land holdings and as such was unequalled for many centuries.

The entry for Hereford provides many fascinating details of life in the city at the time of the Norman Conquest but gives only slight indications of the changes that took place immediately afterwards.

The survey confirms the archaeological evidence that the city had expanded outside its defences. However, the walls still had a function for within them each whole dwelling paid 7^1/2d. while outside they only paid 3^1/2d. This differential doubtless reflected the potential of prime sites in the streets used as markets rather than any security which may have been offered by the defences which, by then, must have fallen into decay. In addition to this tax, the occupiers had to go to Marden for three days in August for reaping, and on one day they had to gather hay wherever the sheriff wished. When the king came to the city, each house had to provide one man to help herd the game if he went hunting. Anyone who was rich enough to own a horse had to accompany the sheriff three times a year to hear pleas and to go to the hundred meet at Wormelow.

Certain people had to make additional payments; thus any man's wife who brewed ale had to pay 10d., while each of the six smiths had to pay 1d. for their forge. The smiths also had to make 120 horseshoes from the king's iron for which they were paid 3d. They then had the advantage of being exempt from any other service.

Hereford possessed a mint and there were seven moneyers in the city, one of whom worked for the bishop. When the currency was being renewed, they had to go to London to collect the dies and pay 18s. for them and another 29s. to the king within a month of their return. They provided the king with as much money as he required, from his own silver, when he arrived in the city.

Coins of William the Conqueror (1066–87) from the Hereford mint

In addition there were complex conditions regarding inheritance and the sheriff, or his deputy the reeve, was empowered to collect all the dues. Before the Conquest they paid a total of £12 to King Edward and £6 to Earl Harold (the Normans never accepted Harold as King of England).

Three crimes are mentioned – breach of the peace, house-breaking and highway robbery. Anyone who committed any of these paid a fine of 100s. to the king.

The effect of the Conquest in Hereford and the surrounding area may well have been greater than that in many other towns. This was largely due to the rapid actions taken by King William in an attempt to protect his vulnerable western border. William FitzOsbern, a close friend of the Conqueror, was made Earl of Hereford and given supreme powers in the border area from Chepstow in the south to Ludlow in the north.

By 1067, William FitzOsbern had started to build or refurbish a series of castles along the western extremities of his lordship. A line of castles, from Chepstow in the south, through Monmouth, Ewyas Harold and Clifford to Richard's Castle and Ludlow in the north, gave Hereford better protection from the Welsh than it had ever enjoyed previously. In addition, the Conqueror pursued a policy of conciliation with the Welsh Princes. As a result, the years following the Norman Conquest were ones of relative peace and prosperity which led the way to a period of development.

FitzOsbern saw Hereford as the heart of his defensive system. As a result of the agreements with the Welsh, Hereford could safely expand outside the line of its early defences and the northern line, at least, was completely abandoned. The land which lay to the north of the Saxon defences apparently belonged to Bishop Walter before the Conquest. Afterwards, Earl William gave the bishop the manor of Eaton Bishop and land at Lydney in Gloucestershire in exchange for 'land in which the market is now' – presumably the new market place which was created in the present High Town and its surrounding area.

The market place laid out by William FitzOsbern is still a significant feature of the City of Hereford. In many ways it was similar to the one at Breteuil on the southern frontier of Normandy – a borough which also belonged to FitzOsbern. The central part of the market was the large triangular area now bounded by Commercial Street (formerly Bye Street) on the north, Union Street on the east, and St Peter's Street on the south-west.

The roads which approached the new market, which supplanted those going through the Saxon town, were designed to widen out as they approached the central triangle. The road from the west is now

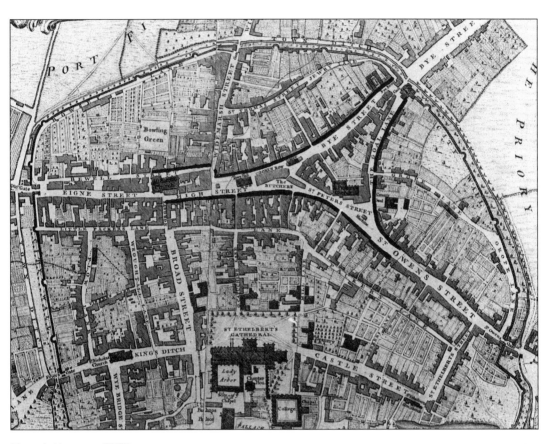

The probable extent of William FitzOsbern's grand market place superimposed on Taylor's map of 1757

represented by Eign Gate Street, but originally probably encompassed the whole area between that street and Bewell Street. To the north-east the approach road is still reflected by the wide Commercial Road, and to the south-east St Owen's Street has a similar aspect.

Accepting the limits as described above, this market place was designed on a vast scale – indeed High Town can be seen as the gradually widening approach road from the west rather than the whole area of the market. Gradually the flimsy stalls, which would have been an original feature of the market place, became more permanent structures. Eventually they would have had living accommodation on upper floors. The main triangle is now filled with buildings as is the area between Eign Gate Street and Bewell Street. The High Town area was similarly filled with buildings until they were gradually demolished during the early years of the nineteenth century.

The creation of the new market place had a permanent effect on the old Saxon town. With the exception of Broad Street, which led down to the ford across the Wye and continued to be a main thoroughfare, the other streets, and particularly the west–east road (King Street to Castle Street), lost much of their importance. It was then practicable to extend the ecclesiastical precinct to the north and thus provide room for the large new cathedral which was to replace Athelstan's minster, probably damaged during the Welsh attack in 1055.

FitzOsbern's new market place was not constructed for the benefit of the citizens of Hereford – it was intended as a new town to be populated by French settlers. The Conquest was followed by an active period of colonization with French knights, monks and tradesmen dominating and exploiting the local populace. The encouragement to come to Hereford was basically a tax advantage as the Domesday survey clearly shows. While the English were left with their former customs, the new French burgesses 'have all their forfeitures discharged for 12d.' (apart from breach of the peace, house-breaking and highway robbery). This was a much lower rate than was charged in other parts of the country, doubtless because of the proximity of the Welsh border, and must have been a very attractive inducement for the new arrivals.

To accommodate the new settlers the land around the new market placed was laid out with parallel plots of land of uniform width and length. At the rear of the plots there was often a back lane. These narrow 'burgage plots' are a standard feature of most post-Conquest settlements and could well be a Norman import. The excellent map of Hereford produced by Isaac Taylor in 1757 shows how well these narrow plots survived into the eighteenth century. The plots on the north side of High Town have Maylord Street (then St Thomas Street) as their back lane and can be seen to have continued outside the line of the later city defences. Similarly, on the north-western side of St Owen's Street, plots of equal length are bounded by Gaol Street (earlier Grope Lane) and once again continued beyond the late twelfth century defensive line.

Burgage plots are not present on the north side of Bewell Street because, as archaeological excavations have shown, this area had already been colonized in the late Saxon period. The south side of Eign Gate Street, High Town, and St Owen's Street backed on to the disused Saxon defences which included a water-filled ditch. Although the ditch stayed in use for many years as an open sewer, the burgage plots all continued back to the road which ran along the inside of the disused defensive embankment. This is now West Street and East Street (earlier Behind-the-Wall Street) which then acted as a back lane.

Taylor's 1757 drawing of St Nicholas' church which almost filled the junction of Bridge Street and King Street. It was demolished in 1842

St Nicholas.

The only formal means of access from the old town to the new market place was through the North Gate in the old defences at the top of Broad Street. Provision was made between various burgage plots for additional passages across the defensive line and some of these still survive. The northern part of Church Street, the Booth Hall passage, Barroll Street, and the recently widened Offa Street still serve a useful purpose as they did when they were laid out over nine hundred years ago, doubtless with flimsy bridges crossing the disused Saxon ditch.

Earl William's new town was an unqualified success. By 1086, the city was paying the king, who then held Hereford in lordship, £60 – a substantial increase on the £18 paid at the time of the Conquest considering that the taxation rates for the original inhabitants had not changed. Most of this increase must have been due to the 12d. payments made by the new French settlers.

The church was an important element of the new Norman settlements and although Hereford had St Guthlac's and the cathedral, the new town had its own parishes based on several new churches. There was only one church, apart from the cathedral, in the Saxon city. This was St Nicholas built in the wide part of the present King Street at its junction with Bridge Street. Its foundation date is unknown.

The first new church to be built is likely to have been All Saints, deliberately positioned in the new market place opposite the old gateway into the Saxon city. It was probably founded by William FitzOsbern for his French settlers very shortly after the Conquest. FitzOsbern did not live long enough to see all his ideas carried out to fruition. In 1069 he returned to France and was killed in an ambush some two years later. His son, Roger, was involved in an unsuccessful attempt to depose the king in 1074 and as a result other interests took over in Hereford.

One of these was Walter de Lacy, who took a leading part in the development of the city after 1075. He was responsible for building the church of St Owen outside the east gate of the Saxon city. He made use of the triangular piece of ground between the defences, the old road which led eastwards and the new road (now St Owen's Street) leading from the market place. He was also responsible for the foundation of St Peter's which he richly endowed with lands in Herefordshire and Shropshire. This was built in the southern part of FitzOsbern's grand market place and may well have included residential quarters to the north of the church, for it started its life as a collegiate church. Walter de Lacy tragically fell to his death from the battlements of the church during a visit in 1085.

CHAPTER FOUR

Castle Green

H ereford castle, once described as being 'as great circuite as Windesore' is now a public open space with no recognizable castle buildings surviving. However, its secrets are not completely hidden, for during exceptionally dry weather regular parched strips of grass begin to appear which have been shown to reflect buried stone foundations. They indicate not just the buildings of the castle, but also the foundations of the pre-Conquest St Guthlac's monastery.

The first castles built in England date to just before the Norman Conquest. Hereford was probably one of the earliest, being built by Ralph, the son of the Count of Vexin and nephew of Edward the Confessor, before 1052. Hereford was then of considerable royal and military importance due to its position close to the Welsh border, and Ralph was made Earl of Hereford and probably installed a Norman garrison in his new castle. The precise location of Ralph's castle is not known but it may well have been of typical motte and bailey design. If this was the case, the motte may still survive as Hogg's Mount – the high point at the north-eastern corner of Castle

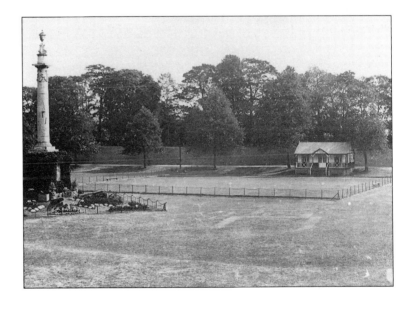

Regular lines which show as parched marks in the grass of Castle Green indicate the position of buried foundations of long lost buildings (Watkins)

Green. This site would have been next to the eastern gate of the city and north of St Guthlac's precinct in an area which probably had relatively little previous use.

The new castle did not last long for, together with the town and cathedral, it was sacked and burnt in 1055 by the Welsh led by Gruffydd ap Llewellyn. There is no record that Harold Godwinson repaired the castle after the sack as he did the defences, and the site may well have been neglected until the Norman Conquest eleven years later.

King William then appointed William FitzOsbern, Lord of Breteuil in Normandy, as palatine Earl of Hereford. The extent of FitzOsbern's work on the castle of Hereford is not known but, at the very least, he must have been responsible for rebuilding Ralph's castle if, indeed, he did not reconstruct it entirely. Edric the Wild is recorded as harassing the garrison of the castle in 1067 so it must have been rebuilt by that date.

The Domesday survey records that St Guthlac's had lost much of its holdings of land after the Conquest and it is evident that this ancient monastic settlement was no longer a great power in the city. As a result it would have been possible for FitzOsbern to build the large motte which stood to the west of the Castle Green and join it, with a northern rampart, to Hogg's Mount. If this was the case, then the new works, together with the Saxon city defences which still survived on the east of the Green, would have completely isolated St Guthlac's monastery and the city cemetery within the new castle boundaries without infringing their land ownership.

Stone was not available in the immediate area of Hereford and it is likely that both early castles were built of timber, the mound being surrounded by a palisade and ditch and crowned with a wooden tower.

Following FitzOsbern's death and the attempt by his son, Roger, to depose the king, the castle of Hereford was forfeited to the crown. Throughout the rest of its history, with one or two minor exceptions, the castle was a royal stronghold, the sheriff normally being responsible for upkeep and repairs.

There are no records of any work on Hereford castle throughout the reigns of William Rufus and his brother Henry I. Although Henry had nominated his daughter, Matilda, as his successor, the Council disagreed and offered the throne to Stephen de Blois, a grandson of the Conqueror. The problems caused by this uncertainty about the succession were to have a dramatic effect on Hereford and its castle.

In 1138 the royal castle was garrisoned by Geoffrey Talbot on behalf of Matilda. By this time the castle was strong enough to withstand a siege by Stephen for five weeks, but during that time the city certainly suffered. In two separate fires 'all below the bridge over Wye was burned down' followed by 'all the other side of the Wye'. A year later war came to Hereford again but this time the castle was in the possession of the king's men. Miles of Gloucester joined forces with Talbot and prepared for a second siege of the castle. According to Robert de Bec, one of Stephen's adherents, Talbot was quite ruthless 'entering into the church of the episcopal seat, dedicated to the Mother of God, and irreligiously driving away the ministers of God's table, he rashly introduced a company of armed men, and turned the house of prayer, the place for the propitiation of souls, into a den of war and blood'. Bec goes on to describe 'the citizens in tears uttering loud cries, either because the burial-place of their friends was thrown up against the ramparts of the castle, and they saw the bodies of their relations, some half putrefied, others very lately buried, drawn without remorse from their graves; or because on the tower, whence they used to hear the sweet and peaceful summons of the bells, they now saw engines erected and missile weapons thrown against the king's men'.

With Talbot bombarding the castle from the cathedral tower and Miles attacking from 'another side', it would appear that the king's forces had retreated to the great motte and eventually they had to surrender. The burial place which was disturbed was presumably the one on Castle Green which surrounded St Guthlac's monastery.

As a result of its precincts being 'polluted with blood', arrangements were made to find a new site for St Guthlac's monastery outside the city and the move took place about 1144. Several buildings, including a late eleventh-century church, which was partially excavated in 1960, were left for the use of the castle's inhabitants. The monks must even have abandoned their patron saint's tomb, for it is recorded that, during the reign of Edward I, when the whole area was within the royal castle, there was a fire which destroyed the wooden shrine which had covered the saint's remains.

Once the monastic settlement had been abandoned, the burial ground doubtless fell into general disuse in favour of the one around the cathedral. However, people do not quickly forget where their ancestors are buried and it was interesting to find that most of the later burials found during the excavations were infants or very small children, all in shallow graves. It is probable that this was a late reuse of the cemetery for illicit burials in what had once been consecrated ground. It could have been an unanticipated result of the royal licence obtained by the Dean and Chapter in 1398 allowing them to enclose the cemetery which then surrounded the cathedral. This was to prevent 'the secret burial of unbaptized children, and the mischief done by

swine and other animals that dragged the dead bodies from their resting place in the ground.'

Throughout the latter part of the twelfth century and the first half of
the thirteenth the royal castle received almost continual attention. Parts
of the castle were being built in stone by 1181 when a lime-kiln was in
use. The great keep on top of the western mound, described as having
'one great towre' encircled with a wall including ten semicircular
towers, was probably built at the beginning of the thirteenth century.
About the same time a 'small tower' was built at a cost of £100.

King John and his successor Henry III were regular visitors to the
city and doubtless occupied the state apartments in the castle. The
castle buildings were not all on the mound – a contemporary description gives an impression of the large number of building that were in
the bailey, now Castle Green. There were the king's great hall, the
king's small hall, chambers for the king and queen and their knights,
the county hall, an almonry, a counting house, a stable, two gaols, an
exchequer chamber, a building in which siege engines were kept, and
the usual offices (kitchen, bakery, etc).

In 1233, Henry had a 'fair and becoming chapel' built onto his
chamber, and in 1245 work on the royal apartments, including wains-
coting and lengthening of the queen's chamber by 20 feet to include a
fireplace and privy chamber, cost £176 7s. 10d. Further work between
1250 and 1252 cost another £100, but by 1254 there were several serious problems. A survey of that date lists the keep roof as requiring
attention; the steps leading up the motte needing to be completely
rebuilt; the Jews' prison being roofless, and both gates in need of
repair. The sheriff was allowed £60 to carry out the repairs and to
build a quay to protect the riverside edge of the Green from erosion by
the river – a problem which was never completely resolved until 1973.

Although there was no fighting in Hereford, the city featured
prominently in the Barons' Wars, being occupied by the rebellious
barons. After the battle of Lewes in 1264 King Henry and his eldest
son, Edward, were brought to Hereford and kept prisoner in the castle.
Their captor, Simon de Montfort, Earl of Leicester, had by then made
Hereford his main headquarters. He rashly allowed Prince Edward to
take exercise on horseback on Widemarsh Common from where, by a
ruse, he escaped to the safety of Roger Mortimer's castle at Wigmore.
De Montfort and his followers were decisively defeated at the battle of
Evesham in the following year.

Further repairs were authorized during the next decade but they
were mainly of a minor nature, apart from a 'certain chapel' which
was rebuilt in 1283–4 at a cost of £10 5s. 8d. This was the last major

BIRD'S-EYE VIEW
OF
HEREFORD CASTLE,
IN ITS ORIGINAL FORM.

From Speed's Map, Leland's Description, &c. &c. &c.

A bird's-eye view of Hereford Castle drawn from Speede's map of 1610 and Leland's description

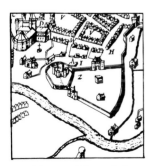

Speede's map of the castle in 1610

project in the castle during the reign of Edward I as his conquest of Wales between 1277 and 1282 meant that Hereford had lost much of its strategic importance. Surveys in 1291 and 1300 indicate a lack of maintenance, and although some work was undertaken in 1307 it was apparently little more than a holding operation. By 1377 the buildings were becoming ruinous and the castle was of such little importance that the Green was let out to pasture.

Renewed disaffection in Wales at the beginning of the fifteenth century led to the Owen Glyndwr rebellion and Hereford castle was once again repaired. Altogether 351 oaks were brought from Haywood Forest and the repair works cost £91 11s. 4^{1}/2d. The great tower was re-roofed, seven watchtowers (presumably those in the wall around the great tower) were repaired, and work was undertaken on the corner tower and the chapel. These defensive works were never used and the castle was once again allowed to fall into decay.

Leland visited the castle a hundred years later and observed that 'the hole castle tendithe toward ruine'. He described the main entrance, which was on the northern side of Castle Green, as comprising 'a great bridge of stone archis, and a draw bridge in the middle of it' although the drawbridge was 'clene downe'. There was also a 'fayre and plentifull springe of water within the castell' and a 'faire chapell' with its east end built 'opere circulari'. This must have been the chapel excavated in 1960 which was found to have a semi-circular apse. The great tower still stood within its encircling wall on the western mound and Leland could still appreciate that Hereford 'hath bene one of the fairest, largest and strongest castles of England'.

The early seventeenth-century Speede map of Hereford shows the castle much as Leland described it. By then there were only two buildings left in the bailey – a square tower and a building presumed to be the chapel. The castle was to have one more short lease of life – during the Civil War some fifty years later.

CHAPTER FIVE

The Defended City

A s development intensified along the southern side of FitzOsbern's Norman market place, the Saxon defences to the rear of the buildings would have gradually been dismantled – the stone from the wall would have been used for new buildings and the earthworks would have been levelled, thus narrowing the ditch until it became little more than an open sewer.

On the eastern side of the city, the Saxon defences were mainly incorporated into the defences of the castle and presumably still lie buried underneath the eastern embankment which surrounds Castle Green. A small section to the north of the castle survived in a ruinous condition behind the medieval defences and has now been exposed at the rear of St Owen's Court.

On the western side of the city the defences probably just fell into disuse – the timber work would have perished, the stone wall would have collapsed in places, and the whole feature would have become completely overgrown. The ditch may well have continued as a watercourse, possibly fed by one of the streams which ran to the north of the city. By *c.* 1125, it is not surprising that William of Malmesbury should have described Hereford as 'not large, but such as appeared by the ruines of broken ditches, to have been something great'.

By the beginning of the twelfth century the castle was the one strong point. The contemporary accounts of the disturbances in Hereford during the troubles of 1138–40 make no mention of any city defences and it was only the castle that was besieged. The city was apparently open to any attack that might take place.

Towards the end of the twelfth century there was increased tension on the Welsh border and in 1195 Rhys ap Gruffydd attacked Painscastle – sufficiently close for the burgesses of Hereford to feel some concern. Although this event may have led the citizens to consider the provision of new defences, many towns and cities in England were being fortified in the 1190s, the reason being more of a commercial nature than strictly for defensive purposes. Once walled and gated,

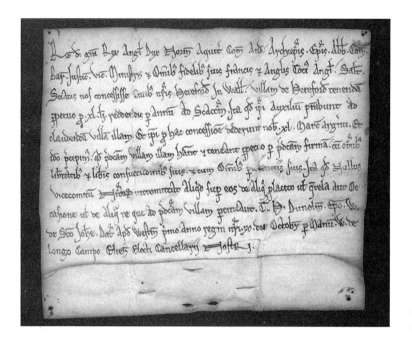

The 1189 Charter given to the city by Richard I

the municipality could obtain powers to regulate and make a charge for traders using the market.

However, the impetus for the construction of new defences in Hereford really came with the granting of the city's first charter. This, given by Richard I in 1189, reads:

Richard by the grace of God King of England Duke of Normandy and Aquitane and Count of Anjou, to the archbishops, bishops, abbots, earls, barons, justices, sheriffs, ministers, and all his faithful subjects both French and English throughout England, greeting. Know that we have granted to our citizens of Hereford in Wales the town of Hereford to hold for ever for £40 to be paid yearly to the Exchequer. So that they shall give help in fortifying the town. And they have give us 40 marks of silver for this grant. And so we order that they shall have and hold the said town for ever for the said rent with all its liberties and free customs with all its appurtenances. So that none of our sheriffs shall impose his administration on them in any plea or suit or dispute or in any matter appertaining to the town.

The intriguing description 'Hereford in Wales' may well be no more than an expression of the remoteness of the city from

Westminster. No doubt the £40 went into the king's coffers to carry on his crusade in the Holy Land. This charter was the foundation of Hereford's independence as an incorporated borough, with the administration of law being carried out by officers appointed by the people. Other charters followed, establishing a Merchant Guild, the right to tax goods brought to market (a grant of murage) and the right to hold a three day fair. The last right still exists – for three days in the first week in May each year the streets of Hereford are taken over with a fun fair.

Once they had the power to enclose the city, the burgesses wasted no time. The old Saxon defensive works on the west side of the city could be reused, and an extension to the north would include the Norman market place and the more central (and presumably more important) burgage plots. The castle provided the necessary defence on the east. In the first instance the new enclosure consisted of an embankment made of material excavated from an external ditch. New gates were needed and the sheriff had an allowance in 1190 of £56 0s. 8d. 'for the making of four city gates, and one gate at the castle'. The new work increased the size of the defended area from the 21 hectares of the Saxon town to a total of 38 hectares north of the river.

Archaeological investigations at the north-western corner have shown that the embankment was about 3 m high and that it sealed traces of buildings and property boundaries of eleventh- and twelfth-century date. There must have been similar infringements of property rights where the defensive line crossed the Norman burgage plots lining Bye Street (now Commercial Street) and St Owen's Street. The loss of property was minimized by increasing the curvature of the defensive line as it approached the main streets. It thus tended to arrive at a right angle to the street, parallel to the long axes of the burgage plots, rather than cutting diagonally across them.

On the east of the city the new defensive rampart joined the Saxon work at right angles – a poor defensive feature. This irregularity, in what was otherwise a relatively smooth curve, was due to the need to keep well away from St Owen's church. The considerable extra length of defensive work which would have been necessary to include the church within the circuit was obviously considered unacceptable. The only alternative was to leave the church sufficiently far outside so as not to compromise the defensive capabilities of the new work.

The new embankment and ditch also truncated the back lanes associated with the burgage plots in Bye Street and St Owen's Street. The sections of the lanes left outside the defences apparently fell into disuse and gradually disappeared.

Bye Street Gate about 1794, copied from a painting by Thomas Hearne in the British Museum. Many small houses and sheds were built in the narrow space between the wall and the ditch

The only gateway in the Saxon defences which was reused was that at the western end of the old main street. Friars' Gate, as it became known in the middle ages, was the least used of the six gates. The main gate leading into the city from the west was Eign Gate, close to the stream that fed the city ditch. To the north was Widemarsh Gate, to the north-east Bye Street or Byster's Gate, while the south-eastern gate – St Owen's Gate – was named after the nearby church. The sixth gate was on the southern end of the bridge that had been built across the Wye. All the gates have now been demolished, but illustrations indicate that they were all rectangular structures and as such they may well date to the construction of the earthwork defences rather than to the later stone walls. Had they been built at a later date they would probably have had semi-circular faces.

Some work took place on the gates in 1216 when timber was granted for the purpose from the Royal Forest of Haywood, just south of the river. A little later, when Henry III came to Hereford in 1223, a fence of brushwood and thorn palings was erected on top of the rampart.

St Owen's Gate in 1784, two years before it was demolished. The building on the left still survives

The outside of Eign Gate, the western entry into the city, in 1784. It was demolished three years later

The first murage grant to the city was in 1224 and may have reflected the inadequacy of the existing defences. The money raised was to be used to face the whole of the defensive circuit with stone and to build or repair the gates. The murage grant was renewed regularly, but even so the work was to take at least forty years to complete. The lack of progress was such that a special mandate was issued to the mayor in 1251 to complete the work. At this time Henry III was waging an increasingly fierce war against the Welsh and was frequently in Hereford where his royal castle was being almost totally rebuilt. In 1262 Llewelyn ravaged Herefordshire as far as Weobley and the burgesses of Hereford must have realized that their city could be in some danger. The work of strengthening the defences in stone was probably completed around the whole 1,645 m circuit by 1265. Hereford was then as strong a walled town as any in England.

The methods used in constructing the wall differed from place to place around the circuit. On the western side, to the north of Friars' Gate, the earlier defences were cut back to a vertical face and a 0.7 m thick wall was built in front of it. Around the northern part of the circuit, the wall was built free-standing on the berm – the space between the rampart and the ditch – and was 1.8 m wide. Along the excavated section, behind what is now St Owen's Court, the foundations, a massive 2.4 m wide, were built into the recut Saxon ditch.

The wall included seventeen semi-circular towers of which two remain. They were apparently built at the same time as the defensive wall and had walls varying from 1.3 to 2 m in thickness. In places, where the wall was built on the berm, the towers had to be built into the face of the ditch.

The surviving Saxon defences, the late twelfth-century gravel rampart, and material thrown up from widening and deepening the ditch, provided a substantial embankment within the wall line. This embankment provided both a fighting platform and an easy means of access around the wall. Several sections eventually became formal roads although other parts were assimilated into the properties which backed on to them. Wall Street, which until recently ran from Eign Gate to Widemarsh Gate, is the most obvious example. The remaining section is now used as the vehicular egress from the Tesco supermarket. Other sections extended the back lanes of the Norman burgage plots that had been truncated half a century earlier. Maylord Street, the lane which ran behind the Bye Street burgages, was extended to follow the rampart and join Bye Street just within Byster's Gate. Sadly, this gradually disappeared during the construction of the ring road and the Maylord Orchards development. However, Gaol Street (originally, and without

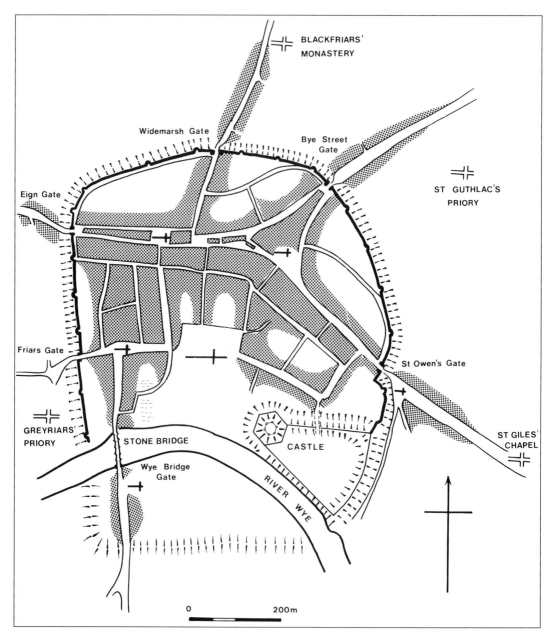

BLACKFRIARS'
MONASTERY

Widemarsh Gate

Bye Street
Gate

ST GUTHLAC'S
PRIORY

Eign Gate

St Owen's Gate

Friars Gate

GREYRIARS'
PRIORY

STONE BRIDGE

CASTLE

ST GILES'
CHAPEL

Wye Bridge
Gate

RIVER WYE

0   200m

Hereford at the end of the
thirteenth century was as strong
a walled town as any in
England

One of the bastion towers near St Owen's Gate in 1804

much doubt appropriately, called Grope Lane) still survives and curves from the back lane of the burgages to join St Owen's Street just inside the Gate position.

An extension to the defences of Hereford was built on the south side of the river to protect the approaches to the Wye bridge and the small suburb of St Martin's. The origin of this bridgehead settlement is uncertain. At first glance, the properties on each side of St Martin's Street, the approach road to the bridge, have similarities to the burgaging in the market area which was laid out after the Conquest.

Demolition of part of the city wall near the site of Widemarsh Gate in 1898. The Wellington Inn now occupies the site (Watkins)

However, Taylor's 1757 map shows a back lane to the east of St Martin's Street but too close to it to allow the standard length of burgage plots. Could this back lane have been the road which led from the south to the ford across the Wye during the Saxon period? The construction of the bridge and its new access road would have led to the owners turning round any properties which fronted the Saxon road to take advantage of the new highway.

Between the two roads, and only a short distance from the river, was St Martin's church. Although the first documentary reference to this building is in 1214, when it was a chapel to All Saints, it is doubtless of a considerably earlier date.

The defensive work which encloses this suburb consists of an earthwork now called Rowe Ditch but originally referred to as the King's Ditch or Wall Ditch. It is still a prominent embankment crossing the meadows opposite the cathedral. The eastern end aligns with the southern corner of the castle on the north bank, while to the west, after crossing St Martin's Street, the embankment turned right to a point on the river bank opposite the main city defences. There is now no trace of either stonework or ditch, but excavations have shown that there was an external ditch which at one time contained stakes set vertically along the bottom as an additional defensive feature. These earthworks are unlikely to be Saxon and may well have been built in 1189 together with the new defences on the north side of the river.

CHAPTER SIX

Religion in the Medieval City

T he residential and business parts of the Saxon city would have changed little in the years after the Conquest. Some trade may have been lost to the new town outside the defences but the general effect was probably minimal, and served to fossilize the old street pattern and its associated, almost square, plots of land. This was certainly not the case with the cathedral and the area surrounding it. By closing the old west–east road, the ecclesiastical precinct could be extended to the north and a new cathedral could be built which would be worthy of the expanding city.

Robert of Lorraine, or Losinga as he is often called, was bishop from 1079 to 1096. He was responsible for the layout of the new Norman cathedral and the beginning of the construction work. William of Malmesbury, visiting in 1135, also accredited Losinga with the construction of a church designed like the basilica at Aix-la-Chapelle. This must have been the chapel of St Katherine and St Mary Magdalene which was demolished, in the face of considerable opposition, in 1737. The deeply recessed doorway on the western side led into two chapels, one above the other, with a central cupola illuminating the upper chapel. The north wall still survives, built into the south wall of the Bishop's Cloister, but it can only be seen from the Bishop's Palace garden.

Did the construction of the cathedral and the chapel involve the immediate demolition of Athelstan's minster, which may have been damaged by the Welsh in 1055? There would hardly have been sufficient room for it to survive had it been between Losinga's chapel and the new cathedral, in the area of the present Bishop's Cloister. Nor was it likely to have been south of Losinga's chapel, where the Bishop's Palace stands. A site for Athelstan's cathedral close to the Vicar's Choral would seem to be the only alternative to at least partial demolition before Losinga started the new work.

The plan of the new cathedral was fairly conventional, consisting of a cruciform building with a central tower and an east end terminating

Taylor included a view of
Losinga's chapel on his 1757
map with the comment 'now
taken down'

in three semi-circular apses. The whole plan apparently took some
fifty years to complete, partly due to the troubles following the death
of Henry I when the tower was used in the attack on the castle. It was
some time before 1148, during Bishop Robert de Bethune's episcop-
acy, that the new cathedral was finally dedicated, in the presence of
six other bishops.

By 1234, the east end had been remodelled with the addition of the
Early English Lady Chapel. This was followed by the construction or
rebuilding, if it had actually been completed as part of the original
plan, of the north transept, which was completed in the 1260s. The
new cathedral and the major additions which followed would then
have provided the focal point for the development of the surrounding
area.

The Bishop's Palace occupies the space between the cathedral and
the river. The earliest part of the present building comprises the great
hall built by Bishop William de Vere in the latter part of the twelfth
century. In its original state it was a four-bay aisled hall with a side
porch and an end chamber block facing the river. The hall, 55 ft wide
and 100 ft long and open to the roof, was certainly appropriate for use
when the bishop had to entertain the king and his retinue during their
regular visits to Hereford.

By 1144 at the latest, following the removal of St Guthlac's from
the castle bailey, the only burial ground for the city was in the area
immediately adjacent to the cathedral. Beyond this would have been
the canonical houses, each presumably in its own grounds. The positions of two are known approximately – when the Vicar's Choral
quadrangle was built in 1472–5, it occupied a vacant plot on which

A mid-eighteenth-century view of Hereford from the south-west. On the left is part of the city wall; the bridge is shown before it was widened, and the cathedral is complete with its western tower and spire

had stood the house of the late Canon Wolston and the ground and house of the late Canon Greene.

The barn at the north-east corner of the present Close is also of great antiquity. It was built in the thirteenth century, possibly with aisles and a scissor-braced roof, and could well represent another canonical hall. By this time the Close must have become well established and the old west–east road completely forgotten.

Most cities became hosts to a variety of religious communities and Hereford was no exception. St Guthlac's, the pre-Conquest foundation on Castle Green; and St Peter's, the de Lacy intrusion into the market place were two of the earliest.

After the troubles of 1138–40, when it was apparent that it was time for St Guthlac's to move, the opportunity was taken to carry out some reforms. The event is recorded in the Gloucester Cartulary:

> Bishop Robert united the church of St Peter of Hereford, situated in the market place, and the church of St Guthlac, unsuitably situated within the circuit of the castle itself, and brought them

Part of the roof of the twelfth-century Bishop's Palace (Watkins)

together with all their private possessions and dignities to form one church, and by his authority as bishop consecrated it for the perpetual service of the Lord as the church of the apostles St Peter, St Paul and St Guthlac, built by him from its foundation outside the city in a place most suitable for religion.

St Peter's in the market place became purely and simply a parish church, but the new foundation received additional endowments rising

This barn, at the north-east corner of Cathedral Close, was built in the thirteenth century, possibly as a house for one of the canons (Hoverd)

to some importance and becoming a regular Benedictine monastery. The new site was to the north-east of the city adjoining the road to Worcester. The buildings have long since disappeared, but shortly after the 1539 dissolution the following description was written:

> The site itself on the north side of the city without Biesters Gate very pleasant and large with much land, spacious gardens and orchards, fine walks (walls?), a small rivulet running under the walls called Eigne, the buildings large and great stately chambers and a large melancholy chapel built with many descents into it from the ground and then of a great height in the roofs struck the enterers with a kind of religious awe.

The communities of religious knights were also represented in the city. The Knights Hospitallers of St John of Jerusalem had a cell of the great preceptory at Dinmore, founded in the second half of the twelfth century, well outside the medieval city in Widemarsh Street. The chapel survives as part of the Coningsby Hospital and is open to the public.

The Knights Templar had a round church, similar to the one surviving in Ludlow Castle, some distance from the city in St Owen's Street adjoining the junction with Ledbury Road. The foundations were discovered in 1927 when a later chapel was being demolished. Although the remains could not be preserved in their entirety, a section survives as part of a garden wall on the junction, with a plaque: 'The stones

The stone foundations of the twelfth-century, round Knights Templar church at the corner of Ledbury Road and St Owen's Street in 1927 (Watkins)

Coningsby's hospital and the chapel of the Knights Hospitallers in Widemarsh Street in 1685. The ornate entry on the right led to Sir Thomas Coningsby's town house which had replaced the Blackfriars Priory

below are part of the walls of the twelfth century round chapel of St Giles, found in 1927 when demolishing the chapel of 1682.' In the wall of a nearby almshouse is an elaborate carved tympanum showing Christ in Majesty which must have been part of the round church.

The Dominicans, usually known as the Black Friars, reached Hereford in the mid-thirteenth century and settled on a site in the Portfield outside St Owen's Gate. They were opposed by the local clergy and as they built their church by day, the Canons turned up in force at night and pulled down their work. The dispute continued for many years until, in 1319, Edward II granted them a new site outside Widemarsh Gate. They gradually consolidated their land holding and built a church and priory within a walled precinct. Edward III completed the work and, together with his son, the Black Prince, three archbishops, one bishop and his confessor, attended the dedication ceremony for the new church. The royal confessor died during the ceremonies and was the first of several notables to be buried within the church. The house had a considerable reputation during Richard II's reign when three successive priors occupied the post of royal confessor. The priory was dissolved in 1538 when there were a prior and seven friars. The inventory included a pair of organs, two bells in the steeple, two sacring bells, two alabaster tables, a large number of vestments and a fireplace in the chapel.

Part of the cloister of the Blackfriars Priory in the mid-nineteenth century. The round stair tower was part of the conversion to a town house for Sir Thomas Coningsby

Part of the cloister survives, having been reused as a town house by Sir Thomas Coningsby in the early seventeenth century. However, the most important reminder of this religious community is the elaborate preaching cross, the only one of its type to survive in England. It stands in a public garden, just off Widemarsh Street, together with the remains of Coningsby's house.

The Franciscans or Grey Friars were also responsible for setting up houses, mainly in cathedral cities and county towns. Their site at Hereford, which had been established by 1250, was outside the defences on the north bank of the Wye, some distance upstream of the Wye bridge. Within the church Owen Tudor (the grandfather of Henry VII) and many local notables were buried. An impression of the house can be gained from a post-dissolution description. The priory was apparently then split into two parts: John Younge had 'a hall called the Hostrye, with two chambers adjoining, under other chambers . . . one garden lying on the west part of the said hall, and one piece of land lying between the wall of the city and the convent orchard', while Walter Nott received 'one great hall and four chambers, lying together under the chambers demised to John Younge, and the common kitchen there, with a garden adjoining, and a bake-house and one stable, and a house called the Gardener's, and one piece of land lying between the said bake-house and stable, and the water-course . . .'. All the buildings have now disappeared but excavations some years ago indicated that the chancel of the church was some 14 m wide and had an elaborately tiled floor.

The Jews came to England shortly after the Norman Conquest as an

The Blackfriars Preaching
Cross in 1830, before the
restoration by Sir Gilbert Scott

offshoot of the French Jewry. They settled in many of the prinicpal cities of the country, first in the rich south-east and then further afield, until they finally arrived in Hereford by 1179. For some thirty years the settlement was small and relatively insignificant, but it rose to considerable prominence in the 1220s due to one member, Hamo of Hereford. The importance of the Hereford Jewry was well demonstrated when Hamo died in 1231, for his heirs had to pay the king one third of his estate – the enormous sum of £4,000. This fine, and pardons granted by the king to people who owed the Jews money, led to a decline in the fortunes of Hamo's heirs who had lost everything, including their house, by 1253.

The Hereford Jews, who lent money mainly to the local barons, had property in Maliarstret (Maylord Street), Vydemareys (Widemarsh) Street, and the Jewry. There was at least one stone house, presumably belonging to Hamo, and a synagogue. The position of the Jewry is a little uncertain but it may well be related to the later Jewry Lane (the eastern part of Maylord Street where it curved, just within the city wall line, to Bye Street Gate) as shown on Taylor's 1757 map.

The Hereford Jews continued to lend money, but on a much smaller scale to local traders and business men, until their expulsion in 1290.

CHAPTER SEVEN

The Middle Ages

During the twelfth and thirteenth centuries, Hereford had been one of the most important cities in the country – not in terms of its population, but because of its strategic position on the Welsh border. The king's castle, the city walls, the important Jewry, and the regular visits from royalty were all expressions of this importance, but it all came to an abrupt end in 1282 when all hopes of Welsh independence were lost with the death of Llywelyn ap Gruffudd. The construction of the Edwardian castles in Wales meant that strong bases along the border, such as that at Hereford, were no longer required.

As a result, by the beginning of the fourteenth century Hereford would have had to accept its position as a rather remote market town, only tenuously joined to the rest of England by roads which were almost impassable for much of the year. Although the consequences of the conquest of Wales must have been a serious blow to the economy of the city, much worse was to follow.

The world-wide epidemic of bubonic plague during the mid-fourteenth century became known as the Black Death. It reached England in August, 1348, and within the year had arrived in Hereford. Throughout the country perhaps a third of the population perished as a result of the epidemic. The plague germ was carried by fleas which lived normally on rats, and in the cities, with stagnant ditches, open sewers, and refuse left in the narrow streets to rot, the death toll could well have been much higher than in the country as a whole. In the Hereford diocese, the episcopal registers tell us that 'It swept away half the population'.

The 'pestilence' came back to Hereford again before the town had time to recover from the first visitation. This was during 1361–2 when the number of deaths was apparently of the same order as had occurred some twelve years earlier. Before the Black Death arrived, the population of Hereford was probably just under 3,000; after the double epidemic it may have been little more than 1,000.

At the beginning of the first outbreak, Bishop Trilleck arranged for the shrine of St Thomas Cantilupe to be carried through the city streets in an attempt to curtail the plague. In 1362, his successor, Bishop

The White Cross, built a mile
west of Hereford by Bishop
Charleton during the second
outbreak of the plague in 1362.
This engraving shows the cross
before its restoration in 1864

Charleton, took a more pragmatic approach and arranged for the market to be held on the city boundary rather than in the streets. At the chosen spot, over a mile to the west of the city centre, he erected a cross with his shield-of-arms carved in panels on the pedestal. The city has now expanded beyond the White Cross which survives, somewhat precariously, in the middle of a traffic roundabout. The pedestal and steps are original, but the shaft and cross were added during the restoration of 1864.

One effect of the plague would have been a vast increase in the number of unoccupied buildings in the city. It would have taken a generation or more before there was any substantial improvement in the population figures, and empty buildings tend to deteriorate very rapidly. Towards the end of the fourteenth century, some thirty years after the plague, it is therefore not surprising to find that new buildings were being erected in the city.

The few which survive to the present day are now some six hundred years old. Houses at that time were mainly set back from the street frontages and as a result have tended to become lost behind newer buildings. In the fourteenth century the main part of the house was the large hall, open to the roof. Attached at one end would be a solar block with the private chambers for the family. The kitchen was often a separate building due to the danger of fire.

Hidden down a narrow passage on the western side of the Bridge Street is a recently restored timber-framed building, now used as offices for a firm of architects. This was built in the last quarter of the fourteenth century, probably as a solar wing to a hall which has long since disappeared. The cusped braces and the carved doorhead on the passage elevation give a slight impression of the considerable decoration which would have been used in a building of this period. The heavily jettied building on the opposite side of the passage is some two hundred years younger than 41a Bridge Street!

The canons' houses, which originally surrounded the Cathedral Close, were the luxury buildings of their period. One of them, 20 Church Street, was built about 1400. It still occupies grounds of considerable size just to the north of the present Cathedral Close. The original building, now hidden behind later brick walls, consisted of a three-bay, first-floor hall with a crown-post roof which was built above a low, ground-floor undercroft. Until recently, the roof was hidden above inserted plaster ceilings, and the shape and size was obscured by later partitions, but the hall has now been completely opened up and gives a fair impression of the luxury in which the medieval clergy lived. In addition to the roof, the removal of later

The side wall of the fourteenth-century solar wing behind 41 Bridge Street before the recent restoration (Hoverd)

wall-coverings has exposed ogee-headed doors and windows and a large stone fireplace.

In Harley Court, a narrow passage leading from the Close, number 5 was also a canon's house of the late fourteenth century. Alfred Watkins the antiquarian, who spent the last sixteen years of his life in this building, never saw the extent of the medieval roof. He knew of its existence for it had been recorded in 1884, before being covered up. Since Watkins' death it has been uncovered again and is now part of a private house.

Part of the crown post roof of the Canon's Hall at 20 Church Street, found hidden above a much later ceiling but now exposed (Hoverd)

The late fourteenth-century window arcade in 20 Church Street (Hoverd)

The successful Hereford merchant would build his house behind his business premises, towards the rear of his burgage plot. Although the size would be constrained by the width of the plot, considerable ornamentation would be normal. One such hall has recently been exposed, hidden behind much later shops on the south-east side of Commercial Street. The roof of this small hall, with its cusped and decorated windbraces and trefoil-headed panels, includes a smoke-bay above what would have been a central hearth. Awaiting a sympathetic developer, it is hoped that this medieval hall can eventually be exposed as part of one of the street frontage shops.

In 1392, Henry Cachepolle, a citizen of Hereford, sold to Thomas Chippenham and two others a tenement called 'Bothehall'. Some six months later the mayor and commonalty of Hereford obtained a licence from the king to acquire this building and grounds, worth 60s. annually, 'because they have no house within the castle or city of Hereford in which the sessions of the justices of assize or of peace, or the Pleas of the city can be held'. The site was on the south side of High Town and it is here that the remains of some municipal and merchant guild buildings survive.

The earliest is probably the Booth Hall, which was only rediscovered in 1919 when a chimney stack fell exposing the medieval roof. A comprehensive restoration has revealed the former glory of the roof. Six bays – some 13.5 m (44 ft) long – survive, although there are indications that the building originally extended further towards High

The late fourteenth-century roof of the hall of one of the canon's houses at 5 Harley Court as exposed in 1884

The medieval hall, recently exposed to the rear of shops in Commercial Street (Hoverd)

Town. The first-floor hall had an elaborately decorated roof consisting of alternate tie-beam and hammer-beam trusses. The hammer-beams include figures of angels, facing downwards, on their ends, and cusped wind-braces form arches and quatrefoils in the roof. The ground floor is totally lost but it may have been completely open with the first-floor hall standing on pillars. The Booth Hall passage, which replaced a wider driving-way, is still a right-of-way underneath the historic hall.

Was this building the 'Bothehall' sold by Henry Cachepolle in 1392 or was it a replacement building? One of the earliest examples of a hammer-beam roof in England is that at Westminster Hall in London, which was built in 1380. The Hereford example must have been built within a few years of that date. The name Booth Hall is probably an alternative for the far more common Guildhall. They were originally used by the medieval trading guilds for their meetings, but the names have come to apply to the various buildings serving as municipal halls. It appears that the Hereford Booth Hall was bought by the city for public use, but by the sixteenth century one part was certainly used for trading while another part was used as a prison for freemen.

In 1934, Alfred Watkins recorded 'the final and complete demolition' of a timber-framed building just to the west of the Booth Hall. He described this building as the Freemen's Prison although firm evidence was lacking. Early in 1992, the building between Watkins' prison and High Town was stripped out for refurbishment. Two additional and hitherto unrecorded bays of Watkins' demolished building

Part of the late fourteenth-century roof of the Booth Hall during the 1919 restoration. On the right is one of the hammer-beams with a figure of an angel (Watkins)

have now been exposed. This timber-framed building, which had a jettied front on the east facing the Booth Hall, was originally some 18.3 m long and 6 m deep (60 ft by 20 ft). It was built late in the fifteenth or very early in the sixteenth century and included several timber-panelled ceilings. However, the most significant feature is the very high ground floor ceiling. This indicates that the ground floor was designed as a large hall rather than a series of rooms. It is possible that this building was the Guildhall, which was built by the city in 1490. On completion the city would have been able to relinquish their use of the Booth Hall in favour of the trade guild.

The late fifteenth century seems to have been a period of resurgence in Hereford when several important projects took place. At the cathedral, the vault of the south-east transept was reconstructed and the Stanbury and Audley chantries were built. Of much greater significance was the construction of the College of the Vicars' Choral. Previously the vicars had had a hall in Castle Street (now part of the cathedral school) but had found it 'so distant from the church that through fear of evil-doers and the inclemency of the weather, many of them cannot go to the church at midnight to celebrate divine service'. The replacement buildings, which comprise the College quadrangle, were built between 1472 and 1475 and consisted of twenty-seven two-roomed houses. The corridor or cloister with its ornamental timber roof, which joins the College to the south-east transept of the cathedral, was added before the end of the century. There are no longer any Vicars' Choral, but their College still survives with several parts still in residential use.

It has been suggested that the first bridge over the River Wye at Hereford was built by Milfrith about AD 800 but firm evidence is lacking. A bridge was certainly in place by 1100 when Bishop de Capella helped in its reconstruction. In 1303 Edward I granted timber for its repair, and in 1383 Richard II provided thirty oaks and forty perches of stone for the same purpose after it had been 'broken and destroyed by the force of water'. These early bridges were probably based on stone piers with a wooden superstructure and would have been built at royal command. The present bridge was built in 1490 but a recent survey has indicated that the builders may well have made use of some of the earlier piers. The bridge has six arches and five piers; the third arch from the city side was demolished in 1645 during the Civil War. There was a defensive gateway at the southern end which was demolished in 1782.

The supposed Freemen's Prison just before demolition in 1934. It may have been the city Guildhall, built in 1490 but by the eighteenth century it had become the Blue Boar Inn (Watkins)

When John Leland visited Hereford in the 1530s he found a town which was 'auncient, large and strongly walled, also having a mayne castel hard by the ripe of Wy. . . . The walle of the towne is cumpased with a dyke always filled with morisch water gethering and

The College of the Vicars' Choral in the early twentieth century

descending onto hyt. . . . The waull and gates of Herford be right well maintainyd by the burgesses of the towne.'

The dissolution of the monasteries in the late 1530s probably had little effect on the city as a whole but the destruction of the fulling mills on the Wye by Henry VIII was much more serious. Cloth-making ceased in Hereford and the city suffered 'extreme ruin and decay and was filled with poor'.

The redundant monastic buildings and lands were sold to the local gentry. John ap Rice purchased St Guthlac's Priory where he took up residence. The Blackfriars site changed hands several times before it passed to Sir Thomas Coningsby who had a house there by 1613 and used the stones from the monastery to build the hospital which still carries his name. The buildings of the Greyfriars survived for some years and are shown on Speede's map of 1610. Afterwards they were completely demolished and there is now no trace above the ground.

Well before the seventeenth century the eastern part of High Town had become full of timber-framed buildings. Here was The Butchery

The Market Hall in the western part of High Town, as it was built in the late sixteenth century (drawing: R. Williams)

and Cooken Row. This latter row of three-storey buildings was where the bakers and confectioners plied their trade, with the Catherine Wheel Inn at their centre. Only the Old House (built 1621) survives of all these buildings and is now one of the city's museums.

The western part of High Town once contained one of the most important and impressive buildings in Hereford – the Market Hall built in the latter part of the sixteenth century. It was 26 m long and 10.6 m wide (85 ft by 35 ft), three storeys high and stood on twenty-seven wooden pillars leaving the ground floor open for a market. The first floor contained the assize court and magistrates' chambers and above them were the rooms for the fourteen city guilds, including bakers, barbers, butchers, clothiers, coopers, glovers, tanners and weavers. These trade guilds continued the medieval economic protectionism by excluding all 'foreign' competition from the city.

By the early seventeenth century Hereford was a relatively prosperous county town with a regular market and well-established trade guilds. Its civic pride was well expressed in its new Market Hall and although there had been another epidemic of the plague in 1610, it is apparent that the city had fully recovered. It now had to face a Civil War.

CHAPTER EIGHT

Civil War in Hereford

From 1642 to 1646 fighting took place throughout England, Scotland and Wales with well over fifty important battles, sieges and skirmishes. Charles had been absolute monarch since 1629 but his extravagances and excursions into France led to economic problems and the reintroduction of the unpopular 'ship money' tax. The Long Parliament was set up in 1640 and gradually two parties, Royalist and Parliamentarian – Cavalier and Roundhead – emerged. Charles could not countenance a loss of absolute power for the crown and decided to fight – four years of civil war followed, with both sides dependent largely on the recruitment of volunteers to reinforce the local militias which were under the control of the various county lieutenants. Throughout the war money was a problem and the troops were seldom paid on time – looting was an inevitable outcome.

The Parliamentarian support was mainly in the richer eastern and south-eastern counties including London while the Royalists depended on Wales, the south-west, the Midlands, and much of the north. Hereford was very much a Royalist stronghold although several of the principal families supported the parliamentary interests.

Hereford, in the middle of the seventeenth century, was still largely enclosed within its medieval walls. All six gates were standing, although they had not been used for defensive purposes for many years. The royal castle had been allowed to fall into total disrepair and many of its buildings were in ruins. At the beginning of the Civil War it was described by Lord Clarendon as 'a town very well affected, and reasonably well fortified, having a strong stone wall about it, and some cannon, and there being in it some soldiers of good reputation, many gentlemen of honour and quality, and three or four hundred soldiers, besides the inhabitants well armed'.

However, the city was totally unprepared when the Parliamentary army under the leadership of the Earl of Stamford suddenly appeared outside the walls on 30 September 1642. The Roundheads occupied the city without any resistance and the Royalists fled. Although the Earl of Stamford took up residence in the Bishop's Palace he was not to stay long. He had no money to pay his troops, little food, and no means of getting credit. After some two and a half months the Parliamentarian forces retired to Gloucester and the Royalists regained the city.

Early in 1643 the king sent Sir Richard Cave to secure Monmouthshire and South Wales and to attempt to unite the Royalist forces throughout the whole area. He liaised with Lord Herbert, who was responsible for all the troops in the area, and apparently had some success. Eventually, on 15 April, Herbert and Cave arrived in Hereford together with the latter's small force of 80 horse and 100 dragoons. Although by this time Sir William Waller and his Parliamentarian troops were close to Ross, Lord Herbert departed from Hereford, leaving Cave effectively as governor of the city and in charge of the Royalist forces.

Cave was very concerned about the lack of any defensive preparations around the city. His advice for improvements to the defences gives a graphic picture of the state of the city at that time – first 'that the breast-work should be made on the bank of the river, upon both sides of the bridge, and that the way under the castle, being upon the same bank, very plain and open as any highway, should be likeways strengthened with a good worke and turnepike, to hinder any entrance by land under the castle, or by water in boats'; secondly 'that a breast-work should be cast up to defend the entrance into the castle by the mill, as plain and open a place as the other, only there is a small ascent'; thirdly 'that deep trenches, with any moveable bridges, until drawbridges could be provided, should be digged and made within every open gate'; fourthly 'that Byster's Gate should be dammed up'; fifthly 'that some old houses in severall places on the wall, should be taken downe'.

However, the citizens of Hereford were not enthusiastic and when the mayor arranged for the common bell to be rung (the summons for the citizens to appear) very few or none came. Even the imminent threat of plundering had little effect and the only work carried out was the 'damming' of Byster's Gate.

Sir Richard Cave could only discover some five barrels of powder in the city – far too little for an effective defence against Sir William Waller and his army. They were approaching from Ross and early in the morning of Tuesday 25 April Cave went to the castle where 'it beginning to be light, the enemies whole forces were discovered to be within lesse than a mile of the towne'. Cave, by drum and trumpet, attempted to get his troops from their lodgings to their posts, but meanwhile the enemy approached nearer and nearer 'both in the ditches and under the hedges, and in the suburbes about the town, beganne to shoot on all parts'.

The attackers started to use boats to ferry their musketeers across the river but they were beaten back. By this time the enemy was just outside Widemarsh Gate with their cannon. This Gate and the nearby Eign Gate were defended by no more than 'a little iron chaine, knee-high, on the outside'. The alternatives were a desperate sally or an honourable treaty. The latter was agreed and, while some of the horse and dragoons marched away to safety, Cave went to Widemarsh Gate to treat. He found that the cannons had been used to shoot through the Gate and 'scoure the street' and rapidly agreed to parley. The initial terms were unacceptable with Cave declaring that 'wee ought every man to dye in the place rather than yield to such conditions'. Negotiations continued and, as news of the proposed treaty filtered

Widemarsh Gate shortly before its demolition in 1798. Cannons were fired through this Gate to 'scoure the street' in 1643

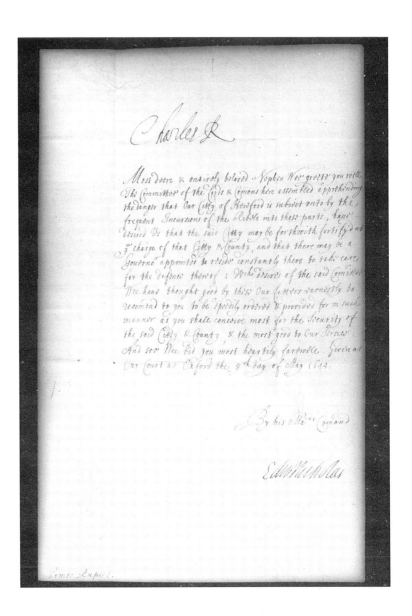

A letter from Charles I written from Oxford in May 1644, concerning the defence of Hereford.

around the city, the Royalist troops gradually left rather than surrender. Eventually a treaty was signed and the Roundheads entered the town, confining the gentry to their lodgings for eventual transfer to Bristol.

Sir Richard Cave managed to escape, helped by an alderman's son, 'over the towne wall, and through the mote, which was not over my bootes'. He rejoined the king at Oxford where he was put under arrest and charged with 'dishonourably giving up the city of Hereford, after it had been entrusted to his care'. He attempted to justify his actions and to lay the blame for the poor showing of Hereford on the general lack of cooperation. His defence was perhaps a little doubtful – Waller discovered some forty barrels of powder in the city which Cave could not explain away! His eventual fate is unknown.

Sir William Waller and his army did not stay long in Hereford and it was soon reoccupied by the Royalists and strongly garrisoned by Barnabas Scudamore. There are some indications that late in 1644 the Royalists operated a mint in Hereford as they did in several other cities under their control.

After the June 1645 defeat of the Royalist army at the battle of Naseby the king retreated to Hereford where he stayed twelve nights. The Civil War was almost over but a few strongholds, including Hereford, still remained loyal to the throne.

A few days after the king left, on 30 July, the Earl of Leven, commander-in-chief of the Scots auxiliaries, arrived on the south side of the river and by the next day had invested the town on all sides. They called for surrender, but Scudamore had had time to put the defences of the city into relatively good order and it was well prepared to defend itself.

Scudamore had taken many of the steps recommended by Sir Richard Cave including pulling down houses outside the walls. Joyce Jefferies in her account book for the period was quite prosaic about it:

> Paid for work donn in making bullwarks to
> defend the Citty of heriford fro invasion .   20d.

> Rece of Maud Pritchet half a yeere's rent for
> her howse in Widemarsh streete, due at
> Holirood day, 1645, being the last that ever she
> paid, for she removed, and my howses were
> pulled downe.   30s.

It is apparent that the townsfolk had had a complete change of heart and were solidly behind Scudamore and his defence of the city. Several sallies took place across the Wye bridge and during one of them one side of St Martin's church steeple was demolished – the church was an asset to the attackers as it was a potential danger to Wye bridge and the Bishop's Palace. The Scots army continued to attack Wye bridge and severely damaged the gate on the southern end. The defenders stopped it up with woolsacks and timber, and when this was unsuccessful they broke out one arch of the bridge and built a strong work behind it.

By 11 August the attackers had resorted to mining below the walls in the Friars' Gate area – one mine was stopped by a countermine and

The Wye bridge in 1685 shortly after the Civil War. The ruins of the Bridge Gate are apparent on the right

another was defeated by the defenders sallying forth and firing it. A few days later four cannons were used against Friars' Gate – a breach was made but was instantly stopped up – a cannonball survives embedded in the wall to this day!

There was a successful sally at St Owen's Gate on 17 August at which time 'little boys strived which should first carry torches to fire their works'. In anger the Scots army turned their batteries against St Owen's church, just outside the Gate, and destroyed it.

A few days later the defenders once again attacked the Scots mining works near St Owen's Gate. Some they fired, suffocating the miners, others they flooded, drowning those which the fire had not consumed.

Every possible means was used to confuse Leven's forces – 'what frequent alarums we gave them by fire-balls, lights upon our steeples, by dogs, cats, and outworne horses, having light matches tyed about them and turned out upon their workes; whereby we put the enemy in such distraction, that sometimes they charged one another'; 'one morning, instead of beating reveillie, we had a cry of hounds in pursuit after the train of a fox about the walles of the citty'.

On 2 September the unsuccessful besiegers heard that King Charles was advancing from Worcester and, in Barnabas' words 'the Scotch mist began to dissipate, and the next morning vanished out of sight'. The Parliamentarians lost at least 1,200 men, the defenders just 21. This was to be the last success for the king; he made Hereford his headquarters for a few days but left later in the month, never to return. During his stay he knighted Barnabas Scudamore and several others and added to the arms of the city a bordure of St Andrew's crosses and the motto *Invictae fidelitatis praemium* – 'The reward of invincible loyalty'.

Hereford's freedom from Parliamentary control was only to last for a few months – the Royalist cause was to become increasingly desperate following the loss of Bristol in September 1645.

The final act of Hereford's part in the Civil War occurred in December 1645. Colonel John Birch had been active in the conquest of Bristol and had been appointed governor of that city and of Bath. However, he wanted to display his ability with a resounding military success and, soliciting help from his many friends in London, was successful in obtaining a commission to 'distress the city of Hereford' with a force of some 1800 horse and foot.

Birch moved his men to Gloucester where he conferred with the governor, Sir Thomas Morgan, and Sir John Bridges. They advised that the scheme was impossible. By then it was middle winter – the roads were poor and travel would be difficult. The whole county had suffered from being ransacked by the Scots army in its quest for food, horses and provisions and would be hostile. Birch listened and disagreed. He persuaded Bridges to accompany him in secret into Herefordshire, a county he had never visited before. At a remote farm near Ledbury they met two ex-Royalist officers, Captains Alderne and Howarth, who provided the essential information to enable Birch to plan a successful attack on Hereford.

He established that the garrison, of horse and foot, totalled some 1,500 and that there was a strict guard kept at night. However, after the gates were opened in the morning the soldiers went drinking, often leaving no more than ten on guard. The officers drank and gambled all night and slept until noon. Birch also discovered that there was sufficient cover for a small force in the ruins of St Guthlac's priory, close to Byster's Gate, and a hiding place for the remainder of his force in a hollow close by – assumed to be Scots Hole to the east of the city. He also learnt that each morning at Byster's Gate, some men arrived from the countryside to break the ice in the city ditch and others came with carts laden with wood and straw.

Birch was satisfied – an attack was feasible. He returned to Gloucester to collect his men and on 12 December marched them to Ledbury. They started off to Hereford the following night, according to his secretary 'in the deep snowe, where some of your men ended there dayes in the extremity of the ffrost and snowe'. By morning they

The memorial to Col. John Birch in Weobley church

Hope of Resurrection to Eternall Life
Here is Deposited the Body of
Coll: Iohn Birch
(Descended of a Worthy Family in Lancashire)
As the Dignities He arrived at in the Field; and the
Esteem Universally yeilded him in the SENAT=HOUSE,
Exceeded the Attainments of most, so they were but the
Moderate and Iust Rewards of his Courage, Conduct~
Wisdom and Fidelity. None who 'new him denyed him y
Charater of aserting & vindicating y Laws & Liberties of
his Country in War, and of promoting it's Welfare 'and
Prosperity in Peace; He was borne y 7 of Sept 1626
And died (a Member of y Hon:ble House of Comons
Being Burgess for Weobley)
May y 10 1691

were some four miles from Hereford but Birch did not intend to attack
the city that day. He put out misleading information that they were
returning to Gloucester and marched back to Ledbury. This story was
soon passed to the governor in Hereford, and the surprise was total
when the next night Birch once again undertook a march towards
Hereford. It was a night of heavy frost with a covering of snow and the
small army moved so silently that not even a dog barked in all the vil-
lages through which they passed. By morning Birch had the main part
of his force securely hidden in Scots Hole and 150 men with firelocks
concealed in St Guthlac's priory ruins.

Previously Birch had arranged for seven men, one acting as constable,
to be ready at Canon Frome. They were provided with a fake warrant,
pickaxes and shovels and appeared as country labourers. That night
Birch moved them to Hereford to join his troops. Two hours were
spent waiting in the bitter cold in the ruins with 'hope keepeing them
warme'. At last the gates were opened and the drawbridge lowered.
Birch sent the six men and the constable forward and, as they were
showing the officer their warrant to enter, the firelocks rushed

Byster's Gate, successfully
taken by Col. Birch's forces
towards the close of the Civil
War

forward. The seven men laid about them with pickaxes and spades and held the gate for the minute it took for the firelocks to take over, closely followed by the remainder of the force from Scots Hole. Within half an hour the city was taken, with the loss of only ten men. The governor, Barnabas Scudamore, and some fifty of his men, managed to escape across the frozen River Wye.

Parliament was impressed with the news – everyone concerned was rewarded – the fake constable, Berrow, received £100 and was made a lieutenant, and Birch was appointed Governor of Hereford. The stratagem he had used was published as *A New Tricke to take Townes* but even his secretary Roe realized that Hereford would be 'almost as difficult to keepe as take'. Birch moved into part of the Bishop's Palace and started to repair the castle.

CHAPTER NINE

After the War

T he Civil War was over, but the economy of the city was in a desperate state and the effects were to be felt for some time. Two parish churches, St Owen's and St Martin's, had been in the line of fire during the siege and were so badly damaged that they had to be demolished. The arch in the Wye bridge, which had been taken down during the war, had to be replaced with a new, slightly higher arch, and in 1684 further repairs cost over £88. One building which could have been saved was, unfortunately, lost. This was the chapter house, built just to the south of the south transept of the cathedral.

The foundations of the chapter house were laid about 1340, but it was probably not completed until about 1370. The delay may well have been due to the plague, for it was not until 1364 that the Dean and Chapter contracted with Thomas of Cambridge to complete the project. This was fortunate, for Thomas designed a fan-vault of an advanced type, contemporary with that in the cloisters of Gloucester cathedral. The building had ten sides and was 13.7 m (45 ft) in diameter. It was described in 1634, by an early tourist to Hereford, as being 'very fayre, and not much shortt of anye wee yet saw, wherein are ten fayre square built windows of Antique worke in good colours. It is adorned on the walls with forty-six old Pictures, curiously drawne and sett outt.'

During the Civil War the lead had been removed from the roof for re-use in the castle and was not replaced afterwards. Bishop Bisse (1712–21) then removed some of the windows when restoring his palace, and by 1769 it was so dangerous that it had to be demolished. Clearance has exposed sufficient of the foundations to appreciate the shape and size of the building and the south wall still stands up to window sill level.

In 1652 the Surveyor General's office carried out a survey of 'The scyte of the ruinous castle of Hereford' in advance of its disposal. The castle was then enclosed with 'the ruins of an old wall, with divers fortifications built upon the said wall, and without the same; together with a certain dwelling house now standing in the said castle, called the Governour's Lodge, consisting of three rooms below stairs and

Remains of the Chapter House which was demolished in 1769, partly as a result of damage during the Civil War (Watkins)

three above, besides garretts and necessary rooms, with two little rooms adjoining to the said house towards the entering into the said castle; all of which . . . containing by estimate five acres and a half, more or less, we value to be worth per annum £6 10s.' They then went on to describe the keep on Castle Hill 'built of stone, having a rampire or wall of stone, about the same . . . which said tower is now covered with lead taken from the chapter house belonging to the cathedral. All the materials of lead and stone, with the timber of the said keep, we value to be worth, upon the place, in gross £40.' There were also two ruinous buildings in the bailey, one of which had been used for the main guard and the other for quartering soldiers, which were worth £20.

Birch had obtained the castle after the war and eventually sold it to Sir Robert Harley and others for £600 'for publique use and benefitt'. The Harleys then granted it to the Justices of the Peace for the county. By 1653 a 'grate part of the stone of the castle was disposed to the College of Hereford (the Vicars' Choral) to build their new dining room, and somme to the city of Hereford to build the Tolsey' (a building used for meetings). Shortly afterwards 'the gravell of the Castle Mount hath been disposed off by order of Sessions'.

The castle gatehouse was initially refurbished and used to store the county records but it too was eventually demolished. By the mid-eighteenth century the castle bailey had been landscaped, possibly by the curiously named Society of Tempers whose aims were 'the promotion of aimiability and good temper'. The City Council now lease the Green from the Justices and it is laid out as a public park.

The accommodation of the old and infirm had been of some considerable concern during the early years of the seventeenth century. The monasteries were no longer there to look after the poor, and in the years leading up to the Civil War several almshouses or hospitals were founded. Kerry and Williams' were founded by about 1600 and were followed by Lingen's, Weaver's and Aubrey's. The latter was founded in 1630 by Mrs Mary Price who owned property between Wroughthall and Plow Lane (now Aubrey Street and Berrington Street) and left £200 to build six tenements on the site. The attractive row of timber-framed buildings still provides housing for six poor women as it has for over 350 years. A few years previously, in 1613, Sir Thomas Coningsby had adapted and added to the thirteenth-century hall and

Aubrey's almshouses founded in 1630 are still in use (Watkins)

chapel of the Knights Hospitallers in Widemarsh Street, to provide a quadrangular hospital for twelve retired soldiers and faithful servants which also survives to the present day.

Although the need for almshouses increased in the aftermath of the Civil War, it was a few years before there were any additions. In 1665 Price's almshouses were built in White Cross Street, and Williams' almshouses, which were well outside the walls of the city in St Owen's Street and may have been damaged during the war, were rebuilt in 1675. Later rebuildings of early foundations include St Giles', also in St Owen's Street, which was founded in 1290 and rebuilt in 1770, and St Ethelbert's in Castle Street, which was founded in 1225 and rebuilt in 1805. All of these still survive and are still in use.

Shortly after the Civil War the grand jury recorded that 'all the streets and back lanes within ye Citty be very foull and nastye for want of skvengers to keep it Clean and hollsome'. By 1696 Celia Fiennes described Hereford as 'a pretty little town of timber buildings', but she may well have been prejudiced in its favour. Cox, writing in 1700, found that 'the buildings are mean and old, and but thinly inhabited, there not being any staple trade to enrich it, or invite people to go and settle in it. . . . Gloves were the most important manufacture but that is too poor a trade to make a place to flourish.' Defoe agreed, when he visited Hereford a few years later and described it as 'truly an old, mean built, and very dirty city, lying low, and on the bank of Wye, which sometimes incommodes them very much, by the violent freshes that come down from the mountains of Wales'.

At the beginning of the eighteenth century Herefordshire was, as now, a very rich agricultural county. Unfortunately Hereford City, with little or no manufacturing industries and very poor communications with the rest of the country, was unable to take full advantage of the marketing potential. It remained basically a local market town with comparatively little trade with the rest of the rapidly expanding country.

However, this was a period of change, particularly in methods of building. The timber-framed buildings which Celia Fiennes so admired were out of fashion; good building timber was becoming scarce, and bricks were being made in increasing quantities. The handsome Mansion House in Widemarsh Street, built by Dr Brewster in 1697, was one of the earliest to make use of this new building material. The high ceilings of the ground-floor reception rooms, the large sash windows and most of all the symmetrical façade, were the essential features of a town house of this early Regency period. St Owen's

Street and Bridge Street contain several good examples of early eighteenth-century houses using the mellow, local brick.

Many people could not afford to rebuild their houses completely but
felt it necessary to follow the new fashion. The ornate jettied timber
fronts of many early buildings were taken down and replaced with
simple brick walls often inadequately tied into the original building. In
some cases, such as the Black Lion in Bridge Street, first-floor jetties
were underbuilt thus gaining more space within the ground floors at
the expense of pedestrians in the streets. Sometimes floors and roofs
were raised to provide the required headroom but others remained
with the low ceilings of the original timber-framed buildings.

High Town contains several examples which have been recently
restored. No. 27, now a jewellers, includes the substantial remains of a
seventeenth-century building which had a double jetty facing onto a
narrow passage, now well-exposed on the first and second floors. Next
door, No. 26, now a bookshop, has the first-floor ceiling of the living

The Mansion House in
Widemarsh Street built by
Dr Brewster in 1697

The sixteenth-century timber-
framed rear wall of W.H.
Smith's shop at 26 High Town.
Inside the shop the first-floor
panelled ceiling is exposed

room of a sixteenth-century merchant's house exposed within the shop. The large principal bedroom on the floor above is now used as an office, and above that would have been the servants' accommodation in the attic roof space. In Commercial Street, the menswear department of Chadd's department store has a typical eighteenth-century brick front, but inside the low, heavily-moulded ceiling beams are typical of late fifteenth-century buildings. They originally belonged to a row of small shops which opened onto the side passage.

The impressive Market Hall, in the middle of High Town, suffered badly from a modernization scheme in 1792. First the top floor was removed 'to ease the pillars of part of their load', and then the remaining part of the building had Georgian windows inserted and was stuccoed in the worst style of the period. This harsh treatment meant that it lost much of its elevational splendour and 'elegance was sacrificed to utility'. It was finally demolished in 1862, the materials being sold for a paltry £200. Four of the main pillars survive in a summer house at Holmer, and the quarter jacks belonging to the clock are in the city

Although all the city gates were demolished at the end of the eighteenth century, the two statues which stood above Byster's Gate have survived and were recently sold at auction

High Town looking east in the mid-nineteenth century. The Market Hall has lost its upper storey and suffered Georgian windows and the Old House is the sole survivor of Butchers'

museum. The positions of the twenty-seven pillars on which it once stood are now marked out with contrasting paving slabs.

Some of the most dramatic changes to the city came as a result of the Paving, Licensing and Lighting Act of 1774. The Act empowered the inhabitants, not only to pave and light the streets, but to 'pull down projections and remove nuisances'. The first buildings to disappear were the six city gates which were demolished in whole or in part between 1782 and 1798. There were apparently some reservations 'the venerable aspect of the place being injured, without an adequate acquisition of elegance'. The narrow, northern part of Broad Street, which for some seven hundred years had preserved the impression of the north gate to the Saxon city, was widened in 1790 with the construction of a town house for the Duke of Norfolk. Within four years it became an hotel – the City Arms – and is now Barclays Bank.

In 1796, John Price had his own strong feelings about 'nuisances' which should be removed when he wrote 'I cannot help mentioning one encroachment upon the regularity of Hereford, which every man of public spirit ought to contribute something towards removing. This

The Old House, the sole survivor of Butchers' Row, in the mid-nineteenth century

is that portion or houses, which are crowded together in the middle of the town, and known by the name of the Butcher-Row. If this nuisance were removed, the market-place, which is indeed spacious at present, would certainly be one of the best in the kingdom.' He goes on to complain that 'the butchers have their slaughter-houses mostly in the above-mentioned places. Besides the indecency of this, which must be apparent to everyone, the moralist might insist upon the evil consequences to society, from such public exhibitions of cruelty. Children, especially, who are fond of crowding to such spectacles, will certainly not find their dispositions meliorated by so gross a familiarity with death.' Price's wish was eventually granted, but it was not until 1837 that the next to the last building in The Butchery and Cooken Row was demolished leaving, by some strange fortune, the Old House. This, the sole survivor of the many buildings which once filled High Town, now stands in rather self-conscious splendour.

Although many historic buildings were demolished towards the end of the eighteenth century and others were hidden behind plain brick façades, a large part of one historic building fell down of its own accord. This was the west tower of the cathedral which, according to Price, had been 'very injudiciously erected upon arches which were designed originally for the support of the roof only'. He goes on to say 'It may not be improper to inform the reader, that this noble structure, which was 125 feet high, began to give some warnings of its fall,

Hereford Cathedral after the collapse of the west tower on Easter Monday, 1786

about a fortnight before it happened. Notwithstanding which, divine service still continued to be performed, till, on Easter Monday, 1786, about seven o'clock in the evening, the arches giving way, the whole mass instantaneously became a heap of ruins.'

The *Hereford Journal* was a little off-hand about the event, recording that 'the ruins though awful, afford a pleasing view, especially to behold the statues of kings and bishops resting one upon another'. The Dean and Chapter employed the architect, James Wyatt, to carry out the restoration work which involved the loss of one bay of the nave, and the destruction of the Norman triforium and clerestory. Wyatt's plain west front was replaced in the early years of the present century by the present front which was designed by Oldrid Scott, son of Gilbert.

The plain west face of the cathedral can be seen in this intimate photograph of the corner of King Street and Broad Street in the late nineteenth century

CHAPTER TEN

Navigation on the Wye

T he Wye rises on Plynlimmon only a few miles from the source of the Severn. It bisects Herefordshire, entering close to Hay-on-Wye from where it follows a winding, but generally easterly course to Hereford, in the centre of the county. Here it bends to the south and, in a succession of long meanders, gradually falls to Ross and eventually leaves the county near Monmouth. The remainder of its course to Chepstow, where it meets the Severn, is in a deep valley with Gwent on the one side and the Forest of Dean on the other. With good reason, George Borrow described it as 'the most lovely river, probably, which the world can boast of'.

The Romans apparently made much use of rivers for the transport of heavy goods but there is no direct evidence to indicate that they used the Wye to any great extent. However, near Kenchester (*Magnis*), in the National Trust gardens at New Weir some 8 km upstream from Hereford, are Roman remains which may hold the key. Here, two massive buttresses were built into the river bank with flights of steps adjoining them. They were associated with a range of buildings which were sufficiently grand to include at least one mosaic floor and an elaborate octagonal cistern. Was it here that a wealthy Roman merchant lived and unloaded the boats which he used for transporting goods up and down the Wye?

When that portion of the Roman Empire that was Britain came to an abrupt end at the beginning of the fifth century, the military roads started to fall into decay. For several hundred years trade over any distance was minimal and for over a thousand years even the best stretches of the king's highway were little more than tracks, almost impassible during winter and with deep ruts and many potholes throughout the remainder of the year. When heavy goods had to be transported and a river was available, boats were the preferred method.

The lower part of the Wye was certainly used for transporting goods as early as the Conquest, for the Domesday survey records that

The Roman masonry in the river bank at the National Trust gardens at New Weir

40 shillings was received from vessels going up the river to the forest. By 1258 wine was being taken by boat as far as Monmouth and indeed, a medieval Monmouth seal includes a masted ship. Other boats were travelling much further upstream for there was apparently a wharf close to Hereford castle as early as 1256.

The main hindrance to navigation on the Wye was because the river also had considerable potential for other purposes. In particular, weirs were built to provide the necessary power for mills and forges. In 1301 the city of Hereford persuaded Edward I to appoint a commission to examine the weirs, dikes and stakes from Monmouth upstream 'as it appears that boats cannot pass as they were wont'. Before 1527 there had been four mills and weirs on the Wye at Hereford, but they had been demolished by order of the king. However, the Dean and Chapter were given permission to rebuild them in 1555. In addition, the many shallows were used as fords, for until the beginning of the seventeenth century there was only one bridge across the Wye in Herefordshire – that at Hereford.

The River Wye has always been subject to floods caused by the heavy rainfall over the Welsh mountains. The floods inundate large areas of low-lying ground but have comparatively little impact on the city of Hereford because the gravel terrace on which it is built is above the flood limit. However, the open ground to the south of the river, now Bishop's Meadow, regularly floods together with parts of the suburb of St Martin's at the southern end of Wye bridge.

At Hereford the river is some 46.3 m (152 ft) above sea level and between Hereford and Monmouth it falls at the rate of about 0.45 m per kilometre (2.4 ft per mile). Such a gradient meant that boats could only travel in flood conditions unless there were locks to control the flow.

It was not until after the Civil War that any serious efforts were made to control the Wye. The first attempt was of a commercial nature when Sir William Sandys of Ombersley Court and several of his relatives obtained a private Act of Parliament in 1662. The Act empowered them to 'make navigable or passable by barges, boats, lighters and other vessels the Rivers Wye and Lugg and the rivulets and brooks and other watercourses running into them in the Counties of Hereford, Gloucester and Monmouth'. The Act allowed for cuts to be made and paths to be constructed and was considered to be 'most profitable and necessary to and for the City of Hereford for conveyance of coals, fuel and other necessaries'. The eventual intention was for boats to travel weekly from Hereford to Bristol with accommodation for passengers as well as goods.

Sandys had previously carried out works of a similar nature on the much more sluggish Avon where he had used a system of weirs and flash locks, but this was far from being practicable on the fast-flowing Wye.

However, the Sandys family must have carried out a considerable amount of work for in 1669 Windsor Sandys was called to the Hereford Quarter Sessions to pay his rent arrears or the County would 'make an entry upon the locks and other appurtenances for carriage belonging . . . to the . . . river whereby it may be disposed of for the general benefit of the County'. By 1671 the Sandys were beginning to lose interest in the Wye and the Justices were 'desired to find out some agent and undertaker who may repair the Lockes and other places in decay'. Repairs were carried out but maintenance was high and by 1675 it was being proposed that the owners of mills and weirs should be bought out to enable the Wye to become 'an Open and Comon River'. At this time Hereford alone needed some 3,650 tons of coal each year. If it could be transported by river, eight boats would be needed and it would sell for no more than fifteen shillings a ton – half the price charged if it came by road transport.

Although the work carried out by the Sandys made the Wye navigable for a few years, at least as far as Hereford, the works were 'performed so slightly that most of the locks and passages made by them did in a very few years fall utterly to decay and ruin' according to a new Act of 1695. This Act set up a committee to carry out the functions previously granted to the Sandys. The committee consisted of several Hereford and Herefordshire notables including the lord bishop of Hereford, the mayor of Hereford and the bailiff of Leominster and 'their heirs and assigns for ever ' – on paper at least it still exists!

Although the objectives were the same as those in the Sandys' Act, the methods of financing were improved. In addition to the costs being a charge on the local rate in Herefordshire, the committee had the power to borrow money. The money was to be used to demolish all the weirs and mills and compensate their owners. The committee was also empowered to build warehouses and tenements on a site below Hereford castle.

Accounts dating to about 1700 relate to the Hereford weir which was then being demolished:

Taking up the rock below Hereford weir	£2. 12s. 0d.
8 men 2 days work each for work below Hereford weir	16s. 0d.
Work done at same weir	7s. 9d.
Bringing barge to Hereford for drawing the stakes	9s. 0d.
8 boys for gathering stones out of the river	2s. 4d.
Enlarging broach in Hereford weir, being about 6 yards in breadth	£7. 15s. 0d.

The position of this weir is not known, but it was presumably somewhere below the Wye bridge. It may have been associated with the 'Bridge Mill' which the navigation committee was negotiating to demolish in 1698.

The committee was apparently successful in purchasing and demolishing almost all the weirs, but unfortunately this did not have the effect that had been expected. Removing the weirs led to many shallows appearing, doubtless where there had been fords at an earlier date. This led to the Act of 1727 which reversed the previous one and allowed the trustees to build mills and weirs with locks where necessary 'for better effecting and preserving navigation of the river above Ross'.

From this time the Wye seems to have been in regular use. Coal came to Hereford and beyond and the county products, including oak bark (for tanning), cider, wheat, flour and wood, were taken to Bristol. In 1777, for example, downward traffic from Hereford included 9,000 tons of corn and 26 tons of cider.

Cider was, and is still, one of the main products of Hereford and the neighbouring areas. Defoe, travelling through the county in the early eighteenth century found that 'we could get no beer or ale in their publick houses, only cyder, and that so very good, so fine, and so cheap,

Anno Septimo & Octavo

Gulielmi **III.** Regis.

An Act for making Navigable the Rivers of *Wye* and *Lugg* in the County of *Hereford.*

Whereas the free and open Navigation upon the Rivers Wye and Lugg, and the Streams falling into them may be a great Increase of Publick Trade, and a beneficial easie conveyance of Ship-Timber, and a continual Nursery of Seamen for the Supply and Service of His Majesties Navy.

Part of the preamble to the 1695 Wye Navigation Act emphasizing the importance of ship-timber and trained seamen

Wye Navigation.

THE *Trustees of the Navigation of the River Wye are desired to meet at the Swan-and-Falcon, in the city of Hereford, on Wednesday the 21st of October next, at eleven in the forenoon, to take into consideration the complaint of the Barge-Owners, and to carry into force the powers of the act of Parliament enabling them to remove the annoyances and obstructions which impede, or affect the safety of, the said Navigation.*
September 15, 1772.   By order of the Trustees,
     HENRY JONES, Clerk.

The Trustees of the Wye Navigation had to meet regularly to deal with complaints from barge owners about obstructions in the river that we never found fault with the exchange; great quantities of this cyder are sent to London, even by land carriage tho' so very remote, which is an evidence for the goodness of it, beyond contradiction'. By this time some cider could well have been transported in barges for Defoe described Leominster as 'a large and good trading town on the river Lug which had lately been made navigable by Act of Parliament, to the very great profit of the trading part of this country, who have now a very great trade for their corn, wool, and other products of this place, into the river Wye; and from the Wye, into the Severn, and so to Bristol'.

Some cider must have been offloaded at Chepstow in 1786 for Edward Davies to have discovered that:

> No better cider does the world supply
> Than grows along thy borders, gentle Wye.
> Delicious, strong and exquisitely fine,
> With all the friendly properties of wine.

The chained library in Hereford includes the Cider Bible in which 'strong drink' is replaced by 'cider'. It must be assumed that Nicholas Hereford, one of Wycliffe's translators, had had some practical experience of this powerful local brew!

Travelling downstream was no great problem providing that there was sufficient water. The reverse direction was much more difficult. The barges could carry up to 20 tons and were normally pulled upstream by teams of five or six men. In addition they had masts and sails for the occasions when wind power could be used.

Boats advertised for sale in the *Hereford Journal* towards the end of the eighteenth century included:

> A barge of about 17 tons burthen, in excellent repair, together with her sail, covering and side tarpaulins, oars and shafts, complete.
>
> Pleasure boat, easy draught of water, adapted for rowing or sailing, holding 20 persons. Awning with checked curtains, full suit of colours, mainmast, mizzen mast, bowsprit, 2 pairs oars, all sails and rigging; at Hereford.

From time to time schemes for further improving the navigation of the river were proposed, but nothing came of them until in 1809 an Act was passed to enable a tow-path to be constructed between Hereford and Lydbrook. The tow-path was opened in January 1811

A barge or 'trow' being hauled up river by a gang of men in 1778. In the background is the cathedral, still with both of its towers, and the landscaped Castle Green

when two barges, each pulled by two horses, made the journey to Hereford.

Taylor's map of 1757 shows three wharves on the banks of the Wye. The one below the partially removed castle mound was that set up as a result of the 1695 Act and included several buildings, presumably warehouses and small houses for the workmen. It was known as the corporation wharf. An overgrown slip and the stone front to the wharf are all that survive.

A second wharf was on the north bank of the river just below the Wye bridge. Here was the Old Bell Inn, the headquarters of the bargemen. Just above the bridge was the Tenters, an area where skins were dried before being transported down the river.

On the opposite bank, just below the bridge, was the coal wharf – the only one with buildings which still survive in a recognizable state. The earliest building, a three-bay, timber-framed, barn-like structure may have started its life as the 'blewhouse' belonging to a succession of dyers in the sixteenth and seventeenth centuries. Several trusses and a timber-framed wall survive, but the building was extensively

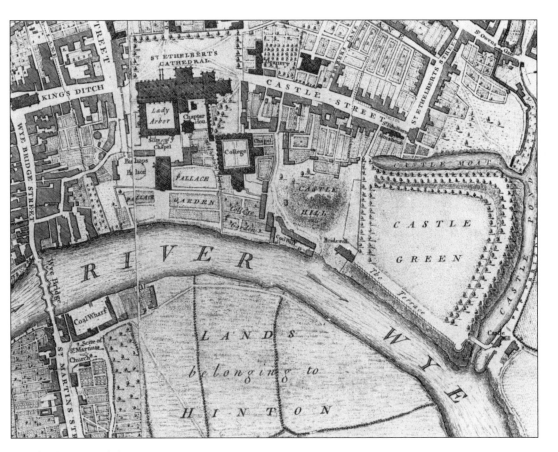

The River Wye on Taylor's 1757 map showing the coal wharves. By this date the buildings in the castle had been demolished, Castle Green had been laid out with formal walks, and the mound was slowly disappearing

renovated, probably about 1700 when its Wye Street frontage was reconstructed in brick. The deep red, almost purple colour and the variable size and contorted character of these bricks indicate that they were made in a coal-fired clamp by brickmakers not appreciating the problems of using fossil fuel.

Western and eastern ranges were added in the eighteenth century using well-fired brick. They enclosed a cobbled courtyard which formed the wharf. Several flights of steps were built up the stone-faced wharf to facilitate access. The buildings had a chequered history after commercial navigation ceased on the Wye. In the 1850s the property was shared between a timber and slate dealer and a coal merchant, but by 1897 it had become the Pomona Cider Company. The buildings fell on hard times by 1945 when they became Nash's sack warehouse. The eastern range and the house adjoining the wharf on the east have both been demolished; the remaining buildings have been empty for over a decade. There are other late eighteenth to early nineteenth

Turner's painting of Hereford Cathedral from across the Wye in 1795. The river is full of activity with a 'trow' in front of the College of the Vicars' Choral

century small warehouses slightly further downstream including one with 'Dorset Ale Stores, Bridport' faintly visible in paint above the doorway.

Hereford was not just a collection of wharves – boats were also built here. As well as the relatively small Wye barges, called trows, there was a boat building yard on Bishop's Meadow where sea-going vessels were constructed and launched. They were built by Mr Easton of Castle Quay between 1822 and 1832 and were sent down the river to Chepstow or Bristol for rigging. Included among them was a brig of 170 tons, 61 ft long and 20 ft in beam, and the largest the brig 'Mary' of 200 tons.

Upstream of the bridge, William Radford's yard built the 64 ton, 14 horse-power, paddle steamer 'Paul Pry' in 1827 for the short-lived Wye Steamboat Company. It was designed for passenger transport with refreshments available on board. The proposed fare to Ross was 4s. and to Chepstow 10s. The boat, which could also pull coal barges, was launched before an audience estimated as six thousand people! However, it only made one trip on the Wye before being sent to Gloucester and eventually Liverpool. A second steamer, the 27 ton, 80 ft long 'Water Witch', was launched with eighty people aboard from Captain Radford's yard in 1834. This was never used on the Wye being sent to Liverpool to be sold.

One of the last boats to be built on the Wye was the 'Wilton Castle', a stern wheel steamer built in Ross in 1902. It was designed to take a hundred passengers at 8 knots on pleasure cruises. It was eventually laid up in 1912 due to a lack of trade.

By the middle of the nineteenth century alternative means of transport had taken over from the Wye trows. The tramway, the canal, and eventually the railway meant the end of commercial transport on the river. The Navigation Acts are still in force and the Wye is now a source of pleasure to the many rowers and canoeists who travel upon it – it remains an important part of Hereford life.

CHAPTER ELEVEN

Solving the Transport Problem

T he coal mines of the Forest of Dean were the nearest source of this essential fuel to Hereford, and by 1801 the city and an area of four miles radius around it consumed no less than 20,000 tons of coal each year. The population of the city was also on the increase, from some 5,600 in 1727 to 6,800 in 1801. Transporting coal up the Wye meant considerable stockpiling to allow for the long periods when the river was too low for barges to make the journey. By the early years of the nineteenth century ways and means were being considered to transport it more cheaply and regularly to the city.

Two totally different methods of transport were available towards the end of the eighteenth century – tramroads, where horses pulled a series of trucks or 'trams' on an iron track; and canals, which were well established in England by this time. Both were considered practicable methods of supplying coal to Hereford and each had its own set of supporters. Both were eventually built, and although they spelt the death of commercial navigation on the Wye, neither was particularly successful.

The first proposal was to build a horse-drawn tramroad from the Wye through the Forest of Dean to the Severn. This had been modified by 1802 to run from opposite Lydbrook to the bridge at Hereford. Nothing came of this scheme, but tramroads were growing rapidly and the South Wales collieries at Blaenavon and Pontypool needed new outlets.

The continuous tramroad which was eventually built from a wharf on the Brecknock canal at Govilon to a new wharf just above the Wye bridge at Hereford was constructed and run by three separate companies. The two southern sections were completed by about 1813, a distance of about thirteen miles to Monmouth Cap.

The final section to Hereford, a distance of some twelve miles, followed at a much later date, apparently due to organized opposition from barge owners and others with vested interests in trade on the Wye. However, the Hereford Railway Company Act received Royal Assent in 1826 and, a sum of £23,700 having been covenanted, work began immediately. It was opened to traffic on Monday, 21 September 1829, when the first coal arrived at the Hereford wharf. Ten and a half tons from this first consignment were distributed among the poor of the city. A fortnight later a public dinner was held at the City Arms Hotel to celebrate the opening.

The permanent track consisted of stone blocks which supported cast-iron sleepers or tie-bars. The plate rails were 4 ft long, 4 in wide with a vertical internal flange 3 in high. The 3 ft 6 in between the flanges was filled with ballast to form a track on which the horses walked. The single-track line included regular passing places. The trucks or trams as they were known consisted of open iron carts, with four 12 in cast-iron wheels, each capable of holding a ton of coal. They were formed into trains and two horses could pull some twelve tons although more were needed on the uphill stretches.

At the wharf in Hereford the Company had a dwelling house, counting house and cottages, with a weighing machine, tram house, workshop and yard. The whole was on a 99 year lease at a rent of £90 per annum. Unfortunately the whole of the wharf and its associated buildings were demolished to make way for the new Greyfriars bridge in 1966. The embankment on which the trams ran still survives in the meadows upstream of the new bridge.

The Hereford Railway Company was underfunded and by 1833 was in debt to the tune of some £6,000. A new manager applied the profits to reduce this debt and by 1846 it was almost completely paid off. Receipts varied between £650 and £1,100 a year, ample to cover the debt repayments and the running costs although it is doubtful if the shareholders received much in the way of a dividend. The running costs were relatively small – salaries for the clerk and collector amounted to £80 per year and upkeep of the track averaged £150. Rents received balanced the cost of the Hereford premises.

In 1845 the Newport, Abergavenny and Hereford Railway Company was formed and eventually bought out the earlier companies, paying £19,460 for the old Hereford Company. The tramway formally closed in May 1853, and although it had only been in operation for some twenty-four years it had ensured that the price of coal in Hereford was reduced to about 22s. a ton delivered into cellars.

In 1774 Robert Whitworth suggested constructing two canals from Hereford: one via Leominster to Stourport-on-Severn, and one through

Hereford Railway.

THE Public are respectfully informed that the RAILWAY from MONMOUTH CAP to the CITY of HEREFORD, will be COMPLETED for the Conveyance of COAL on Monday the Twenty-first of September Instant, and that a sufficient quantity of Coal will on that day by ready for delivery, at the Wharf near to Wye-Bridge, Hereford.

By Order of the Committee of the Railway Company.
WM. PATESHALL, } Clerks.
AND
F. L. BODENHAM, }

A GENERAL ASSEMBLY of the Proprietors of the Herefordshire and Glocestershire Canal Navigation will be held at the Canal Office, in Ledbury, on Thursday the 24th day of September, 1829, at eleven o'clock.
Shareholders are particularly requested to attend, as the best means of completing the Canal to Hereford will be fully entered into at this Assembly.
STEPHEN BALLARD, Clerk to the Company.
Canal Office, Ledbury.

The tramway to Abergavenny and the canal to Gloucester are juxtaposed in these advertisements in the *Hereford Journal*, 9 September 1829

Ledbury to Gloucester. The former route came to nothing, but the mania for constructing canals had arrived and by 1790 a share subscription had been opened for the Hereford to Gloucester Canal at an estimated cost of almost £70,000.

The potential trade from Gloucester and Bristol was listed during the deliberations and indicates the variety of goods which were presumably then being brought to Hereford along the poor roads or by barges up the Wye. They included coal, cheese, ironwork from Coalbrookdale, Birmingham and Sheffield, Manchester goods, tea, salt, pottery, hemp, tiles, glass, bottles, mahogany, wine, spirits – a total of some 15,700 tons. The postulated return trade from Hereford was exclusively agricultural – wool, corn, meal, cider, timber bark and hops totalling 11,500 tons.

An Act of Parliament was passed in April 1791, and work started in the summer of 1792 on the sixteen-mile Ledbury to Gloucester section. This stretch, with a lateral cut to the collieries at Newent, was opened with the customary festivities in March 1798, and the price of coal in Ledbury was reduced overnight from 24s. to 13s. 6d. per ton. The project had cost the Company of Proprietors of the Herefordshire and Gloucestershire Canal Navigation over £100,000 – more than the original estimate for the whole route to Hereford.

The lack of capital and the reluctance of the shareholders to invest any more money into a scheme which showed little likelihood of any return resulted in a lack of any further action for over a quarter of a century. This changed in 1827 when the committee appointed Stephen Ballard as clerk. He was an enthusiastic young man who firmly believed that the completion of the canal was both practicable and financially viable. His enthusiasm was infectious and the necessary Act, for a revised route, was approved in May 1839, ten years after the Abergavenny tramroad reached Hereford. Three years earlier there had been a well-attended meeting in Hereford to discuss a proposal by Isambard Kingdom Brunel for a railway to Gloucester. Although no action followed this meeting, railways were obviously the transport system of the future and canals were set for a rapid decline.

In this climate it is surprising that all the shares in the new canal project were taken up. Ballard acted as project engineer and by 1840 some five hundred men were employed on the work. The canal was opened to Withington, almost within sight of Hereford, in February 1844. A celebratory dinner was held at the City Arms Hotel in Hereford that evening.

The last stretch of the canal involved a tunnel, a quarter-of-a-mile long, underneath Aylestone Hill in the suburbs of Hereford. Work

The terminus of the Gloucester
to Hereford canal – the basin at
Barr's Court in the mid-
nineteenth century

proceeded apace and the basin in Hereford was finally filled with
water on 22 May 1845. There were no celebrations to mark the completion of what was the last mainline navigation to be opened in the
south of England. The canal company were already considering entering negotiations 'with any railway company that might see the eligibil-
ity of treating with this company for the purchase of the canal'.

The Ledbury to Hereford section cost £141,000; the whole canal
had involved nearly a quarter of a million pounds and had taken over
fifty years to complete. From a poor start, confidence was restored
when it was appreciated that the company's attempts to sell the canal
were unsuccessful. Trade grew rapidly from a mere 6,410 tons in 1828
to 43,080 tons in 1848. Surprisingly, the arrival of the railway in
Hereford had little effect – the tonnage in 1858, three years after the
Hereford–Ross–Gloucester line opened, was a creditable 47,560.

The last full year of operation was 1880; the following year the section from Ledbury to Gloucester was closed to allow construction of
the railway joining the two towns. The Ledbury to Hereford section,
with no access to the main waterways, was doomed to fall into obliv-
ion. Alfred Watkins, the antiquarian and photographer, made a final

A stage wagon travelling west
in High Street in 1804

journey on the canal by canoe. In 1880 he and a friend took two days
to travel the full length.

There are only a few traces of the canal remaining in Hereford.
There is still a tunnel under Aylestone Hill, and a bridge over the line
of the canal at the upper end of Widemarsh Street. There were originally three discharging wharves in front of the Barrs Court railway station. The basins have all been filled in and they, and the warehouses
and offices belonging to the canal company, have now totally disappeared.

Before the middle of the eighteenth century the traveller in
Herefordshire had to depend on his horse or on the covered stage wag-
ons which are often a feature of contemporary illustrations. Turnpike
Trusts were set up during the eighteenth century to repair the roads but
were only really effective during the nineteenth century. Even then,
only 20 per cent of the road system was within their jurisidiction. As
late as 1789 there were few highways in the county capable of taking
wheeled traffic once the winter weather set in. The variations in condition depended on the local availability of crushed stone for repair and
in 1805 Duncumb noted that 'the north side of Herefordshire has the
worst public roads; the private roads are universally bad'.

The city had turnpike gates, where tolls were collected, in St
Owen's Street at the junction with Ledbury Road; on the summit of
Aylestone Hill; in Widemarsh Street near the Essex Arms; in both

*For the Conveniency of sending Presents at this Sea-
son of the Year, and for the Quick Conveyance
of Passengers to and from London,*
PRUEN's MACHINES
Will begin FLYING on the following Days
Glocefter Machines,
In One Day, Six Times a Week,
S ET out from the Bell-Inn, in Glocefter, and
the Swan with Two Necks Inn, Lad-Lane, London,
every Evening, (Saturdays excepted) at Eight o'clock.—
Infides 13s. Outfides Half Price.
Hereford Machine,
In a Day and a Half, Twice a Week,
Sets out from the Redfireak-tree Inn, in Hereford, every
Tuefday and Thurfday morning at Seven o'clock, and from
the Swan with Two Necks Inn, Lad-Lane, London, every
Monday and Wednefday evening.—Infides 1l. Outfides
Half-price.

The *Hereford Journal*
advertisement for 'Pruen's Flying
Machine', which took a day and
a half to travel from Hereford to
London in January 1775

THE RAPID.
NEW PATENT SAFETY DAY COACH

TO LONDON.

T HE Public are most respectfully informed,
that this GREAT ACCOMMODATION leaves the
BLACK SWAN INN, HEREFORD, EVERY MORN-
ING, (except Sunday,) at a Quarter before Five, through
ROSS, GLOCESTER, CHELTENHAM, OXFORD,
HENLEY, MAIDENHEAD, and SLOUGH, to the
White Bear, Piccadilly; Black Bear, Burlington Arcade;
Boar and Castle, Oxford-street; Bell and Crown, Hol-
born ; and Bull Inn, Aldgate.
On its Return, leaves LONDON every Morning at 7.
JOHN NELSON,
J. M. ROBERTS, and Co. } Proprietors.

By 1835 there was a daily
coach to London completing the
journey in a day

The Royal Mail and Light
Coaches with only four inside
passengers were the most rapid
means of transport in the early
nineteenth century. This *Hereford
Journal* advertisement of 1827
shows the range of services

Barton station, with a train
about to leave for Abergavenny
and Newport in the 1860s. The
station was closed to passenger
traffic in 1893

Whitecross Road and Breinton Road leading west; and south of the
river at the junction of the roads approaching from Abergavenny and
Ross. They were finally abolished in the 1870s.

A stagecoach was running to London by 1774, taking thirty-six hours
for the journey and costing £1 5s. for an outside passenger. It was not
until 1821 that the journey could be made in a day, leaving Hereford at 5
a.m. and arriving in London at 9 p.m. Coach travel was at its peak in the
1830s when it was possible to travel from Hereford to many regional
centres. As the roads improved, the coaches, with their new elliptical
springs, travelled faster. By the mid-1830s the journey to Brecon took
five hours, Bristol eight hours and Shrewsbury six hours. A new coach,
the Protector, went direct to Liverpool in eleven hours.

Hereford was isolated from the main railway system for several
years and remained dependent on its coaches going first to
Birmingham and, as the railway moved nearer, to Gloucester (for
London); to Newport (for South Wales) and to Shrewsbury (for the
north). The last few coaches continued to run to Worcester until 1861
and to Hay and Brecon until 1863.

Hereford was the last major city in England to be connected to the
railway network. The Shrewsbury and Hereford Railway Act was
approved in 1846 but construction work did not begin until 1850. The
service was open to Ludlow in April 1852, but construction of the

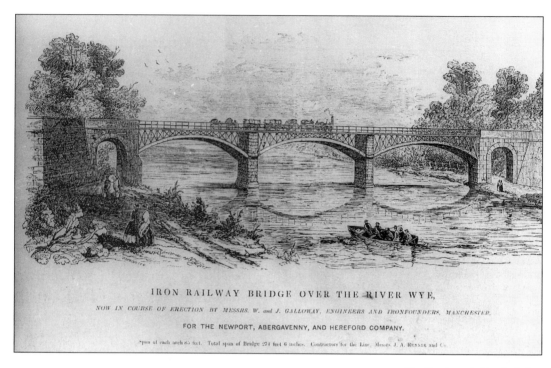

IRON RAILWAY BRIDGE OVER THE RIVER WYE,

NOW IN COURSE OF ERECTION BY MESSRS. W. and J. GALLOWAY, ENGINEERS AND IRONFOUNDERS, MANCHESTER.

FOR THE NEWPORT, ABERGAVENNY, AND HEREFORD COMPANY.

Span of each arch 85 feet. Total span of Bridge 274 feet 6 inches. Contractors for the Line, Messrs. J. A. Rennie and Co.

tunnel underneath Dinmore Hill delayed the arrival in Hereford at Barr's Court Station until 6 December 1853.

Although there was considerable interest in replacing the horse-drawn tramway with a railway joining Hereford to Abergavenny and the growing town of Newport, and the enabling Act was obtained in 1846, finance was limited and it was not until May 1853 that the three tramways closed. The railway finally opened to Barton Station, to the west of the city, on 2 January 1854, crossing the Wye at Hunderton Bridge. The Newport line and the Shrewsbury line were joined by a mile-long loop to the north of the city.

The railway from Hereford to Gloucester via Ross took some four years to construct because of the four tunnels and four crossings of the Wye. It finally opened on 2 June 1855. A two-mile link, from Rotherwas to Red Hill on the south of the Wye, was built in 1866 to join this line with the Abergavenny and Newport railway.

In the 1840s there were several suggestions for a line joining Worcester and Hereford, which was also seen as a link to South Wales, but it was not until 1858 that work started. The tunnels under the Malverns and the viaducts across the Severn and near Ledbury took time to construct and the line did not open to Barr's Court station in Hereford until September, 1861.

The Hunderton bridge, built in 1853 for the Newport to Hereford railway, is now used as a pedestrian and cycle route into the city

Barr's Court station – the terminus of the Shrewsbury to Hereford railway – shortly after opening in 1853. This is the only station to survive in Hereford

The Eign railway bridge, built for the Hereford to Gloucester line in 1855, still takes all rail traffic southwards from Hereford

The last line to be constructed from Hereford was the Hay-on-Wye and Brecon railway. It opened to Eardisley in 1863 and to Brecon in 1864. This railway originally used the third of Hereford's stations, that at Moorfields. However, this station was only used for passengers for some ten years after which the trains were diverted to Barton station. Barton closed to passengers in 1893 leaving Barr's Court as the only passenger station throughout the twentieth century. Both the Gloucester and the Brecon lines were finally closed in the early 1960s.

CHAPTER TWELVE

The Last 200 Years

Although the Lamp Act, as it became known, was the cause of many of the changes to the streetscape in Hereford, with its emphasis on widening streets to allow 'the free circulation of air', several of the more radical proposals fortunately did not take effect. The suggestion to make Church Street into a 'handsome avenue' from High Town to the cathedral was abandoned, and the commissioned architect's preferred choice for the site for a new county gaol – Castle Green – was not acceptable.

Some of the earliest gaols in Hereford were those in the castle which belonged to the king, and those of the bishop, presumably within the palace precinct. Gradually the civil authorities took over responsibilities for the punishment of offenders and, as a result, had to provide their own gaols.

At the beginning of the sixteenth century, and probably for some time previously, the city gaol was in the southern part of Bye Street Gate. It was a notorious place in the late seventeenth century when the gaoler, one William Huck 'a common lewd person, a swearer, curser, liar, drunkard . . . a common hunter of whorehouses . . . murthered one Mary Bar(n)ard, a prisoner, that was under his care . . . by knocking her on the head with the gaol keys'.

The prison continued in use after the Bye Street Gate was demolished in 1798. By 1808 it consisted of several small courts, one containing 'the whipping post' and 'down eleven steps, are two horrid dungeons totally dark (apparently no longer used). Here is also one room, justly denominated 'the Black Hole' which . . . has no light nor ventilation . . . and in this wretched sink-hole was a poor deranged man, in the most filthy and pitiable state'. Following this report the underground cells were abandoned, but the gaol continued in use until the mid-1840s when it was demolished. The City Council replaced it with a purpose-built prison in the renamed Gaol Street (earlier Grope Lane). This prison was closed in 1877 when part of it became the city police station. The building, with its small windows and heavily rusticated exterior, is now used as the magistrates' court.

From time to time the county authorities made use of Castle Cliffe, the only surviving building of the castle, as a Bridewell or House of Correction, but during the eighteenth century the main county gaol was in St Peter's Square where the Shire Hall now stands. This building was examined by the prison reformer, John Howard, in 1782 who noted, among other deficiencies, that drink was available 'as if in a common ale-house'. Apparently there was a window in the adjoining 'Golden Fleece Inn' which 'opened into the first court of the old gaol'!

The County Council acknowledged the deficiencies of the St Peter's Street gaol and decided to erect a new building 'on the plan of solitary confinement recommended by Mr Howard'. The site eventually chosen was in Bye Street (now Commercial Road) where St Guthlac's priory had once stood. After some delay, the Council agreed in 1792 to appoint an up-and-coming young architect, John Nash, to design and build the new gaol. Nash had already designed gaols at Carmarthen and Cardigan and after he finished the Hereford project in 1796 he returned to London to become one of the most fashionable architects of the day.

As with many others of the period, the design of the new prison was based on a central great hall from which ranges of buildings radiated in the form of a cross, the whole being surrounded by a high brick wall. The only entry was in Bye Street, through massive doors in a heavily rusticated single-storey building. Above this entrance was a

The Nash designed entrance to the County Gaol in Commercial Road in 1823. Public hangings were carried out on the flat roof above the entrance for many years

flat roof designed as the place of execution by hanging. In 1816, when this platform had become partly obscured by a pediment, the Gaol Committee recommended that the latter should be removed 'in order that future executions may be fully exposed to the general view of all spectators without the walls, and of all the prisoners within . . . in the hope of preventing crimes by making a due impression on all who witness these melancholy examples'.

Throughout the years the county prison had many alterations and extensions, eventually becoming a detention centre for soldiers. It was closed in 1929 and the City Council bought it for the site value. The

The central octagon and front wing of John Nash's 1796 County Gaol in Commercial Road just before demolition in 1930 (Morgan)

whole of the complex was demolished within a two year period with the exception of the end part of one wing which had been converted into the prison governor's house. The site eventually became the city 'bus station and the Nash-designed governor's house still survives as the Omnibus Office.

Once the new County Gaol was built, the St Peter's Square site was available for redevelopment. The County Council eventually obtained an Act of Parliament for the erection of a Shire Hall, Courts of Justice, and other buildings on the site. The architect was Mr (later Sir) Robert Smirke, who was eventually to design the British Museum. The Shire Hall, which is in the Greek revival style, was completed by 1817. Although no longer used for its original purpose, since the forced amalgamation of Herefordshire and Worcestershire in 1974, it still complements the Square.

The City Council have held their meetings in a variety of buildings throughout their recorded history. They moved from the Guildhall on the south side of High Town, probably when the Tolsey (or Guildhall), shown on Taylor's 1757 map at the Bye Street end of High Town, was built. This was in poor repair in 1768 and meetings were then

The interior of the County Gaol just before demolition. The open door led into the condemned cell (Morgan)

St Peter's Square in the first half of the nineteenth century with the new Shire Hall built in the Greek revival style

transferred to the White Lion Inn in Bye Street. Early in the nineteenth century the Council started to buy property at the corner of Maylord Street and Widemarsh Street where the New Inn stood. The backland area became the Butter Market and towards the street frontage was the Council Chamber and a Guildhall for the courts. In 1882 the Council moved to the Mansion House on the opposite side of the street and stayed there until the new Town Hall was opened in 1904. Standing on the south side of St Owen's Street and surrounded by earlier buildings, this terracotta extravaganza was designed by H.A. Cheers and cost £25,000 to build.

The Lamp Act, which had provided the impetus for the changes which took place in the city during the first half of the nineteenth century was followed by the Hereford Improvement Act of 1854. This led to the provision of mains sewers, and eventually a sewage works; a waterworks providing piped water; and a municipal cattle market, which removed animal trading from the main streets of the city. The first gasworks were built by 1836, and mains electricity was available after 1899. The city was ready to go into the twentieth century.

Throughout most of its recorded history, the few industrial processes which took place in Hereford were associated with agricultural products. When the inner ring road was being constructed in 1967, archaeological excavations unearthed the remains of two seventh-century ovens which had been used for drying grain – certainly the first example of industrial working in the city. The corn mills and fulling mills on the River Wye, destroyed by order of Henry VIII to improve the navigation, were also associated with farming products. Speede's map of 1610 shows two water mills on the line of the city ditch below the castle. There were others around the circuit at various times, and several on the Tan Brook/Eign Brook including one at Monkmoor which belonged to the monks of St Guthlac's.

The production of leather was an important Hereford trade and there were several tanneries in the neighbourhood. They were all built well outside the central part of the city for, in addition to needing large quantities of water, they produced a most unsavoury smell. The mill at Monkmoor had been converted to leather working by the early eighteenth century and others were outside Eign Gate and Friars' Gate. The skins, which came directly from the butchers, had first to be de-horned and cleaned of meat. They were then immersed in pits containing gradually stronger solutions of lime to loosen the hair and any remaining flesh. After further cleaning they were then put into tan pits – containing increasing strengths of a mixture of ground oak bark and water – for as long as eighteen months. Cleaning, oiling and drying in special louvred sheds produced the hides which could then be used by the local shoemaker, cobbler, etc.

Although made for many hundreds of years in the area, cider production reached an early peak in the latter part of the seventeenth century when 'the Hereford orchards were a pattern for all England'. The most famous apple was the Redstreak, developed by the first Lord Scudamore at Holme Lacy, and producing 'a wonderful and refreshing drink'. Defoe appreciated this local Herefordshire drink which still continues to be one of the main products of the county.

Herefordshire is also renowned for its hops which are used in the production of the best of English beers. Hops were first grown in England in the early sixteenth century and two hundred years later 'they plant abundance indeed all over the county, and they are very good' according to Defoe. Before the middle of the nineteenth century most beers were brewed in sheds at the rear of the numerous public houses in the city. This changed in 1858 when Charles Watkins, a local entrepreneur and father of Alfred, started the Imperial Brewery in Bewell Street. He had previously been landlord (and chief brewer) at the Imperial Inn in Widemarsh Street. Products of the brewery included 'Old Household Ale', 'Watkins Cream Stout', and 'Golden Sunlight Ale'. The latter won the only gold medal at an International Exhibition in 1886. When it was sold in 1898, the 'Imperial Empire' included thirty-five hotels and public houses in the neighbourhood as well as the brewery. During the twentieth century the brewery suffered from a series of take-overs as brewing firms gradually grew larger. It was closed and all the

The Hereford Brewery in Bewell Street about 1840. It was bought by Charles Watkins about 1858 when it became the Imperial Brewery. The buildings were demolished in the early 1960s

Radford's Iron and Brass Foundry in Friar Street lasted for only a few years before being converted to a flour mill

buildings demolished in the early 1960s. A large Tesco supermarket now occupies the site.

Captain Radford, who was involved in shipbuilding on the Wye in the early nineteenth century, also built an iron foundry in Friar Street in 1834. The venture was unsuccessful and the works were eventually taken over by Charles Watkins who converted them to a steam-powered flour mill and maltings. Improvements followed rapidly with

The Imperial Flour Mills early in the twentieth century. The front of Radford's Iron Foundry and its tall stack are still recognizable

Nos 2 and 3 High Street at the beginning of the twentieth century

the introduction of the first roller milling plant in the county. The Imperial Flour Mills were also the first buildings in the city to be lit with electricity. The original foundry building still survives although much altered.

 Throughout the twentieth century Hereford has continued to grow. It has improved its position as an important market centre and continues to have the only main road crossing of the River Wye for traffic travelling along the Welsh border. During the first half of the century the main through roads were narrow and the Wye bridge, although it had been widened in 1826, was only just wide enough to take two lanes of traffic. Various solutions were proposed including the demolition of All Saints church and all the properties between Eign Street and Bewell Street to create a wide boulevard. Fortunately this radical scheme was turned down and only limited widening has taken place in the city's streets. Eventually, in the early 1960s, an inner relief road associated with a new bridge over the Wye was approved. Following the line of the medieval city ditch, the ring road was completed in 1968 and has allowed much of the city centre including High Town to be pedestrianized.

 Inevitably, many buildings of historic interest have been lost in the last half century including the Corn Exchange in Broad Street, St Vincent's Orphanage in Berrington Street, the Black Swan in Widemarsh Street and many smaller buildings of seventeenth century and earlier date. One very odd survivor, which constantly surprises the visitor to Hereford, is in High Street. Self-consciously sat on a shelf, half-way up the modern façade of Littlewoods Store, is a remnant of an ornate sixteenth-century timber-framed building. It was moved on rollers into High Town for some months while the new store was built and then returned, although not quite in its original place!

 In 1898 a local guide described Hereford as combining 'in a large degree, the charms of antiquity with the better phases of the spirit of modern progress'. The author went on to say:

> It is scarcely the place, perhaps, for the man of competition and speculation, who is only at home in the hurly-burly of the world, and whose great aim in life is to be the first in the race for wealth; but for him of a contented mind, who can enjoy the harvest of a quiet eye – the artist, the poet, the antiquarian; Hereford may be esteemed as a true Arcadia, a veritable Paradise of the west.

No. 3 High Street being moved
on rollers across High Town
before being hoisted on to a
shelf in the Littlewoods façade

Hereford – Yesterday and Today

Like many towns, the historic centre of Hereford is relatively small – the entire area within the medieval walls being less than forty hectares. The full perambulation described below can take up to two hours, allowing for stops, but short and medium routes are included with return directions at appropriate points. The starting point is the open area in front of the west face of the cathedral.

The Close, to the north of the cathedral, is surrounded by buildings on all sides except the west, where it is open to the junction of King Street, leading westwards, and Broad Street, which goes north towards All Saints Church. In the Saxon period this was the intersection of the two principal roads of the city. At that time King Street continued through the northern part of the Close to form the main west–east road by joining with Castle Street. Broad Street continued to the south to the ford across the River Wye. Nowadays, Broad Street narrows in front of the west face of the cathedral to become Palace Yard which leads, through a timber-framed archway, into the Bishop's Palace grounds. Displayed within this archway are two massive curved timbers which came from the roof of the twelfth-century Bishop's Palace. Others still remain in place as part of the present Palace – the oldest 'house' to survive in the city.

Follow the narrow lane, Gwynne Street, on the right of the Palace entry.

On the right a pleasant row of cottages gives way to a fine, late nineteenth century grain warehouse built in polychrome brick. On the left,

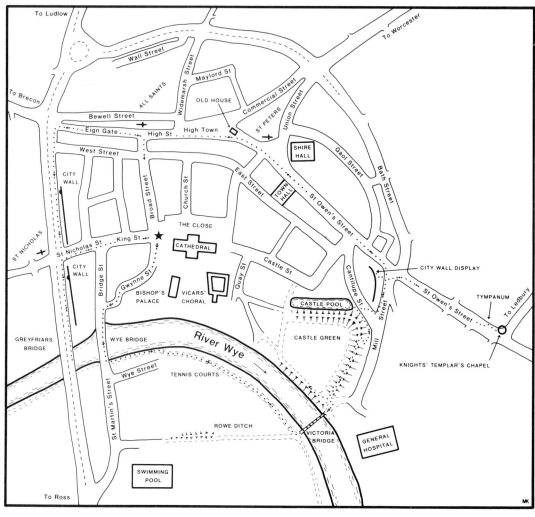

A walk around Hereford – a modern map of the city showing the route

the high stone wall of the Bishop's Palace grounds includes a plaque recording the traditional birthplace of one of Hereford's most famous daughters. Pretty, witty, Nell Gwynne (1650–87) left Hereford when young and eventually gained considerable notoriety as mistress of Charles II. Could she ever have imagined that her grandson, James Beauclerk, was eventually to return to Hereford as bishop?

Continue down the winding Gwynne Street through an archway into Bridge Street.

One of the sixteenth-century wall-paintings in the Black Lion Inn in Bridge Street showing the breaking of the Sixth Commandment (Hoverd)

Across the street is the Black Lion Inn. A fine timber-framed building, this hostelry is notable for the sixteenth-century wall paintings in a first-floor room which unfortunately is not open to the public. They depict the breaking of the Ten Commandments.

Turn left down Bridge Street onto the Wye bridge. First look up river (to your right) and then cross over the road and look downstream. The triangular refuges give some protection from traffic.

The bridge was built about 1490, probably on the foundations of an earlier one. Until 1782 it had a defended gateway at the southern end.

It was widened in 1826 and, until the Greyfriars bridge was built upstream in 1967, had to accommodate all the Welsh border traffic travelling through the city. Downstream, the high retaining wall on the right was the quayside for a coal wharf when barges came up the Wye.

> **Continue across the bridge (noting the traces of a Victorian urinal in the last downstream refuge) and turn left down the riverside path in front of the Lancaster (sadly no longer the Saracen's Head) Inn. Walk to where the path widens and look back to the bridge.**

The Wye bridge was a weak point during the 1645 Civil War siege. To protect the city, the third arch from the town side was demolished and rebuilt afterwards to a different design. Behind you, the various buildings which adjoin the inn were all associated with the navigational use of the Wye. Here coal arrived from the Forest of Dean and the produce of Hereford was stored to await transport to Bristol and around the coast to London. Across the river there was a second quay between the Bishop's Palace garden and the bridge. The ford, which crossed the Wye at this point and after which Hereford is named, may well have been used by the Romans.

> **Continue along the riverside path past the tennis courts.**

Across the river, next to the Bishop's Palace, is the College of the Vicars' Choral. It was built in the 1470s for the twenty-seven residential vicars. The large bay window of the College hall is a prominent feature; the stone came from Hereford castle. The riverside wall downstream of the College is a remnant of yet another coal wharf, and beyond it is the stone-built Castle Cliffe. Originally the Water Gate for the castle, it became the governor's house during the Civil War. It was then used as the Bridewell (gaol) until 1786 when it was converted to a private house. Behind, on the far side of the tennis courts, is a low earthen bank which once defended St Martin's suburb, the part of Hereford to the south of the river.

> **Continue along the river bank to the Victoria suspension bridge (built 1897).**

Hereford castle stood on the high ground opposite. The stone, tower-like structure close to the bridge is not part of the castle. It is a modern construction containing the pumping mechanism to supply water to Castle Pool. Downstream from the bridge, on the far bank, is the General Hospital dating back to 1783. In front of it the shallows are all that remains of the castle ford.

Crossing the bridge, a flight of steps or a more gentle path leads up to the left on to the broad open area of Castle Green.

Castle Green has had a long and fascinating history. Originally it was used as the city cemetery which surrounded the pre-Conquest monastery of St Guthlac. After the Norman Conquest it became the bailey of the royal castle and would have been full of buildings. It was laid out as a pleasure ground after the Civil War. Although the castle has disappeared, during dry summers the lines of long-buried walls can be seen as brown parched marks in the grass. In the centre of the Green, the memorial to Lord Nelson was erected in 1809 – the urn on top of it was the less costly alternative to the planned statue when funds ran out!

Castle Green in the early nineteenth century showing the memorial as originally planned, with a statue of Nelson on top

The short walk can be completed by crossing the Green on the path above the river. Castle Cliffe is now on your left and the landscaped area beyond is Redcliffe Gardens where the castle mound originally stood. The paths lead to Quay Street which curves up into Castle Street. Turn left and through the gates to return to Cathedral Close.

To continue the walk head towards the highest point on the embankment surrounding the Green at the north-eastern corner. Here there is a rather well-concealed flight of steps which leads down to Mill Street. Turn left and continue until Castle Pool is on your left – this was once part of the castle moat – then cross Cantilupe Street, returning to continue up Mill Street. Go through the archway on the left which leads to the rear of St Owen's Court flats. Although it looks private, access is allowed. A fragment of the City Wall is in front of you. Follow it to the right to a breach in the Wall.

Hidden behind St Owen's Court is a unique display of the evolution of the defences of Hereford. The reconstructed timber face is an accurate representation of the late ninth-century defensive work which fronted a clay and turf rampart. Some fifty years later it was replaced by a roughly-built stone wall, erected when the timbers began to give way under the pressure of the rampart. The City Wall in front of the display was built over three hundred years later using the original ditch as a foundation trench

Return through the arch and turn left to St Owen's Street.

An 'out-and-back' diversion is of some interest.

Turn right, following St Owen's Street across the traffic lights, cross the road and continue to where the Ledbury road bears to the left.

Fixed to the garden wall at this corner, and usually hidden behind a wooden seat, is a plaque recording the position of the twelfth-century round chapel of the Knights Templar. This was replaced by St Giles' chapel in 1682 – a building which extended well into the junction.

The display of the Saxon and medieval defences at the rear of St Owen's Court (Hoverd)

Road safety demanded its demolition, and in 1927 it was moved to a new site

> **Returning along St Owen's Street towards the city centre, the first building on the right is St Giles' almshouses. At the city end, go through the gate and look at the side wall.**

Here is a magnificent stone carving of Christ in Majesty, typical of the best work of the twelfth-century Herefordshire School of Carving best known at Kilpeck church. It probably came from the Templars' church.

> **Continue back towards the city, past the seventeenth-century Williams' almshouses and the rebuilt St Giles' chapel and once again cross at the traffic lights, completing the out-and-back diversion.**

The site of St Owen's Gate – the eastern gateway to the city – is now marked with a plaque. It was demolished, along with the other five Gates of the city, in the late eighteenth century 'for the better

St Giles' chapel, built in 1682 and demolished in 1927 (Watkins)

accommodation of the public'. Part of the stone-built porter's lodge, which adjoined the Gate, is visible up the passage on the right.

Follow St Owen's Street into the city towards St Peter's Square.

On the left-hand side is the Town Hall, a terracotta creation which heralded the beginning of the twentieth century. A little further on the right, and facing St Peter's Square, is the Greek revival Shire Hall (built in 1819 to the design of Sir Robert Smirke). In front is a statue of Sir George Cornewall Lewis MP, one time Chancellor of the Exchequer. St Peter's church is on the north side of the Square. The founder, Walter de Lacy, died after falling from its battlements in 1085. The Eleanor Cross in the centre of the Square is the city's War Memorial. Apart from the two world wars and subsequent battles, it commemorates recent losses by the SAS in the Falkland Islands.

Leave the Square along St Peter's Street towards High Town.

High Town was part of the market which was constructed just outside the Saxon defences shortly after the Norman Conquest. There was a church at each end – St Peter's to the east and All Saints to the west.

The twelfth-century tympanum showing Christ in Majesty now in the side wall of St Giles' almshouses (Watkins)

Originally it would have been filled with market stalls but, as time went by, they became more permanent structures and eventually the whole area was filled with rows of timber-framed shops and houses. Most were demolished at the beginning of the nineteenth century and now only the Old House (built 1621) remains as an isolated reminder of Cooken Row and The Butchery.

The most tragic loss was the 1862 demolition of the magnificent Market Hall which stood in the western part of High Town. Built towards the end of the sixteenth century, it contained the magistrates' chambers on the first floor with the fourteen city guilds using the upper storey. The ground floor was completely open for use as a market – the whole building standing on twenty-seven massive wooden pillars. Its position and size can still be appreciated by the rows of contrasting paving blocks which represent the pillar bases.

Leave High Town in a westerly direction towards the narrow High Street.

On the left, the timber-framed remnant of a once important shop sits uncomfortably on a shelf in the front of the modern Littlewoods store.

Continue as far as All Saints' church with its leaning spire.

All Saints' church was built just outside the North Gate of the Saxon city. The Gate, and the bridge which crossed the defensive ditch, sealed this northern end of Broad Street. All above-ground traces of these defensive works have long since disappeared, but foundations built on the soft ditch fill can create problems. Look closely at the façade of Barclays Bank on the left side of Broad Street (built in 1790 as a town house for the Duke of Norfolk). On each side of the door-way the window sills have an appreciable slope – the result of subsidence into the Saxon ditch fill.

The medium length walk can be completed by following Broad Street to the cathedral, passing the imposing Green Dragon Hotel and the City Museum and Library (built in 1874) on the right.

To continue the walk follow Eign Gate Street – the continuation of High Street – to where it joins the ring road.

Eign Gate Street is now pedestrianized, but until the ring road was completed in 1968 it was a busy vehicular thoroughfare taking all the traffic to Kington, Brecon and mid-Wales. Before the ring road was built this junction boasted the only set of traffic lights in Herefordshire! The thirteenth-century Eign Gate stood here and the ring road was built on the line of the city ditch – its outline is marked on the walls in the adjoining subway.

Turn left down the narrow passage called Gunners Lane and follow the footpath on the verge of the ring road towards the next set of traffic lights

On the left is a grassy bank which seals traces of the Saxon defences. It is followed by an excellent stretch of the thirteenth-century City

Wall including one of the semi-circular towers. When the wall was complete there were seventeen of these towers – only two remain. Towards the end of this section of wall there is an iron cannonball of Civil War vintage firmly embedded in the masonry. The traffic lights mark the position of Friars' Gate which provided access into the city for the Franciscan monks (Greyfriars) who had their house outside the walls. To the right of these traffic lights is the nineteenth-century St Nicholas' church.

Continue straight ahead on to the approach to Greyfriars bridge.

Low down on the left is the second surviving City Wall tower, complete with arrow slits. From the middle of this new bridge there is an excellent view of the old Wye bridge with the cathedral in the background. Looking upstream, the long, straight stretch of river is in regular use for rowing races. In the distance, the Hunderton railway bridge (built 1854) is now used only by pedestrians and cyclists.

Return to the traffic lights and turn right along St Nicholas' Street to the junction with Bridge Street.

The original St Nicholas' church almost filled this wide open space until its demolition in 1842. There was barely room for traffic to pass the building in any direction, severely restricting access to the Wye bridge.

In the late eighteenth and nineteenth centuries many timber-framed buildings were refaced in brick and their earlier history is now hidden behind the façades. A narrow passage, a few yards down Bridge Street on the right-hand side (next to No. 41), is an excellent example. On the left is the massive jetty of a sixteenth-century merchant's house, while on the right, the small independent timber-framed building dates back to the fourteenth century and was probably the solar wing of a long-lost medieval hall.

Return to the junction and continue along King Street, the continuation of St Nicholas' Street, towards the cathedral.

The eastern end of King Street in the late 1920s. The buildings at the end of King Street were demolished in 1935

There is now a long, open view of the cathedral and Close, but until 1935 several buildings provided an end piece to this street. Up to that date the cathedral could only be seen through the entrance passages to the Close, providing a more intimate setting for this noble building.

On Easter Monday, 1786, the west tower, west front and the adjoining parts of the nave and aisles of the cathedral fell down. The new face was plain, and it comes as a surprise to many visitors to discover that the present more decorative west face was built in the early years of the twentieth century.

The Next Steps

There are several museums which illustrate various aspects of the history of the city. The opening times may vary from those mentioned below.

City Museum and Art Gallery, Broad Street. Natural history, archaeology and local history. Open Tuesday–Saturday and Bank Holiday Mondays.

Old House Museum, High Town. Furnished in seventeenth-century style. Open Monday–Saturday.

Churchill Gardens Museum, Aylestone Hill. Furniture, costume and paintings of eighteenth & nineteenth centuries. Open Tuesday–Saturday, Sunday (summer) and Bank Holiday Mondays.

Cider Museum and Cider Brandy Distillery. Comprehensive display of cider making through the ages. Open April to October daily; November to March, Monday–Saturday. Pre-booked parties at any time.

The Coningsby Museum, Widemarsh Street. Thirteenth-century building used as period museum. Open Easter to September daily except Monday and Friday.

Bulmer Railway Centre, Eign Street. Locomotives and rolling stock. Open Easter to September, weekends and Bank Holidays only. Special open days when 'in steam'.

Broomy Hill Engines, Broomy Hill. Herefordshire waterworks museum. Open Bank Holidays and some Sundays. Usually 'in steam' on Bank Holidays.

Hereford Cathedral: Crypt, includes Mappa Mundi and Diocesan Treasury. Open daily.

Hereford Cathedral: Chained Library, books and manuscripts from the eighth century. Open daily.

For those who want to carry out more detailed research involving books, maps, plans and original documents there are:

The Local Studies Section, County Library, Broad Street. Local books, prints, photographs etc. Open Tuesday–Saturday.

The County Records Office, Harold Street. Historical and genealogical research. Open Monday–Friday. Booking essential.

THE WOOLHOPE CLUB

The Woolhope Naturalists' Field Club, which was founded in 1851, is also the Antiquarian, Archaeological and Local History Society for Herefordshire. It publishes a yearly *Transactions* which is, without any doubt, one of the most rewarding sources of information about the city of Hereford.

The individual articles in the *Transactions*, which have been consulted in the preparation of this volume, are far too numerous to list. The County Library and the County Records Office both hold full sets of the *Transactions*, and the Local Studies section of the library includes copies of most, if not all, of the works in the following list.

This list contains the most important published sources of information about the city including those which are still in print.

GENERAL WORKS QUOTED IN THE TEXT

The Itinerary of John Leland, ed. L. Toulmin Smith, 5 vols, 1908 (reprint 1964). New edition in modern English to be published early 1993 (Alan Sutton Publishing)
A Tour through the Whole Island of Great Britain (Daniel Defoe), ed. P.N. Furbank and W.R. Owens, 1991

THE CITY

The Book of Hereford, J.W. and M. Tonkin, 1975
Domesday Book, Herefordshire, ed. F. and C. Thorn, 1983
Yesterday's Town: Hereford, D. Whitehead, 1983
'Historic Towns – Hereford', from *Historic Towns, Vol 1*, ed. M.D. Lobel, 1969
Hereford in old picture postcards, D. Foxton, 1983
Hereford 800, a celebration, ed. A.E. Sandford, 1989
Outlines of old and new Hereford, W. Collins, 1911
Historical Landmarks of Hereford, W. Collins, 1915 (Facsimile, 1990)
Hereford in Old Photographs, A. Sandford, 1987

Hereford, Then and Now, Vols 1 and 2, D. Foxton, 1988 and 1991
Victoria History of the County of Hereford, Vol. 1, 1908
Collections towards the History and Antiquities of the County of Hereford, J. Duncumb, 1804
An Historical Account of the City of Hereford, J. Price, 1796 (Facsimile, 1970)

ARCHAEOLOGY

Archaeology of the Welsh Marches, S.C. Stanford, 1991
Hereford City Excavations: Vol. 2 – Excavations on and close to the defences; Vol. 3 – The finds, R. Shoesmith, 1982 and 1985
Excavations on the site of the Romano-British town of Magna, Kenchester, Herefordshire, Vol 1, 1912–13; Vol. 2, 1924–6, 1916 and 1926
'Credenhill Camp, Herefordshire; An Iron-age Hill-fort capital', S.C. Stanford, *Archaeological Journal*, Vol. 127, pp. 82–129, 1971

THE CASTLE

The History of the King's Works, ed. H.M. Colvin, 1963
Hereford City Excavations, Vol. 1 – Excavations at Castle Green, R. Shoesmith, 1980
A short history of Castle Green and Hereford Castle, R. Shoesmith, 1980

CIVIL WAR

Memorials of the Civil War . . . as it affected Herefordshire, 2 Vols, J. Webb (ed. T.W. Webb), 1879
Military Memoir of Colonel John Birch, J. Webb (ed. T.W. Webb), 1873
Roundhead to Royalist – A biography of Col. John Birch, E. Heath-Agnew, 1977

TRANSPORT

The Hereford & Gloucester Canal, D.E. Bick, 1979
Early Railways between Abergavenny and Hereford, R.A. Cook and C.R. Clinker, 1984
Hereford and Worcester Railways remembered, L. Oppitz, 1990

BUILDINGS

*An Inventory of the Historical Monuments in Herefordshire: Vol. 1 –
    South-west*, Royal Commission on Historical Monuments, England,
    1931
The Buildings of England: Herefordshire, N. Pevsner, 1963

OTHER WORKS

Herefordshire, Woolhope Club, 1954
The River Wye, K. Kissack, 1978
Alfred Watkins, A Herefordshire Man, R. Shoesmith, 1990
A Pocketful of Hops, Bromyard and District Local History Society,
    1988

Index